How To Build A Daily Self-Discipline

Daily Blueprint To Cure The Procrastination, Laziness, Develop Your Mental Toughness, Achieve Your Goals Faster, And Change Your Life With Simple Atomic Habits.

By

Mind Building School

Table of Contents

Introduction

Congratulations on purchasing *How To Build Self-Discipline For a Successful Business*. The book is a special guide towards helping you achieve your goals faster, become a successful business person and improve your life by learning a simple daily discipline.

In the following chapters, you will find answers about why building self-discipline is important beyond the entrepreneurship and business world and the beauty of owning your business. You will find information that will help you build a successful business entity and achieve the autonomy, independence and financial security. You will find helpful tips and tools on how to begin the journey of self-discipline. When mastered effectively, these tips and tools can set you on a path to greater success not only as a business person but also in your individual life.

There are plenty of books on this subject on the market, thanks again for choosing this one! Every effort was made to ensure it is full of as much useful information as possible, please enjoy!

Welcome
THE FUTURE
IS NOW

Chapter 1: An Introduction to Self-Discipline

The Beauty of Owning a Business

The journey to financial independence and security is long and arduous with no guarantee of success. While some opt for employment to reach their destination, others opt for business ownership while a good number of people settle for both. For those who decide to join the seemingly perilous journey of investing in a business as their gateway to achieving their financial goals, the rewards are usually bountiful with the right frame of mind and strategic thinking. Successful ownership of a business requires a mental steeliness, unmatched commitment, dedication, and strategic thinking that only a self-disciplined individual can achieve.

Many commentators and articles have supported a school thought that business ownership and self-employment is a journey riddled with unending pitfalls and setbacks. However, these articles and commentators fail the objectivity test. They view the issue from a subjective and rather biased point of view. Whether informed by personal experiences or those of others, such a view fails to highlight how great it is to own your own enterprise. This book seeks to counter the assertions of the naysayers who constantly exaggerate the pitfalls. While underscoring the benefits of owning a business, the book will also help you start the journey towards business ownership by equipping with valuable self-discipline tips.

One of the perks that come with owning your business is being your own boss and having the controls to steer your destiny to the direction you desire. This especially comes in handy for Type A personalities who like to be at the center stage of decision making. Individuals who thrive in decision making positions and like taking control are more suited to the life of being a business owner. With your business, you more or less don't have to follow directions and instructions from other bosses.

Working for yourself can help you live a more satisfying life since you get to decide key issues such as working hours and a sphere of professional interactions almost on a daily basis. You get to decide when to take a vacation and monetary rewards. For those who are more inclined towards leading and not leading, owning a business can give you the opportunity to express your leadership skills.

However, being your own boss does not necessarily mean you are immune from taking directions from others. A business is built a mesh of connections and interactions that creates what is known as a business network. A business network can include employees, governments, institutions, distributors, suppliers, customers, and other businesses. These different entities, in one way or the other, determine the success of any business. The beauty of it all is that you have a greater say in all decisions in spite of the choices they might present to you.

One of the challenges faced by many people is striking a balance between work and life. Work-life balance is a determinant of quality of life. Many families and social ties have been broken because of the failure to find this elusive balance. Inability to strike balance the two is one of the leading causes of divorces, social reclusion, depression, and stress among employees. When you own a business, you are more likely to operate with a flexible schedule and hence a flexible lifestyle. If you are a parent, you don't have to miss all your son's evening baseball games in the name of work. You can slot in such vital responsibilities within your schedule with a lot of ease because you are your own boss. Whether you are retired, owning a business gives you a chance to engaging in other more satisfying activities while also securing your financial future.

Owning a business also comes with the benefit of financial growth and stability. The many self-made billionaires who started small and grew their businesses into multi-billion empires are a testament to financial gains associated with business ownership. Most of the individuals who make the Forbes' list of wealthiest people in the world started their journeys from scratch. The success stories of Microsoft, Apple, and many family-owned businesses provide proof that owning a business can sometimes come with truckload of money, literary.

Moreover, these success stories also point to a different non-financial benefit: contributing to local and global economies. From offering employment opportunities to creating new, innovative, and transformative ideas, entrepreneurship has historically played a vital role in shaping our societies. Owning a business gives you the chance to be part of something bigger and greater than you. It offers you the chance to transform lives, improve quality of lives, and contribute to a bigger picture. Your seemingly small business is part of the collage of life.

Entrepreneurship has been at the forefront of transforming our societies for many centuries. Modern-day civilization including technological revolution that is currently sweeping across the globe is founded on business ownership or entrepreneurship. World-renowned entrepreneurs such as Bill Gates of Microsoft, the late Steve Jobs who co-founded Apple, Mark Zuckerberg of Facebook, and Jeff Bezos of Amazon made a name for themselves by taking the plunge in the seemingly murky waters of business ownership. Their successes have had far-reaching consequences in many global communities beyond creation of employment for millions of people. They have also used the resulting wealth to enhance the quality of lives of many people through philanthropic contributions. Annually, they contribute billions of dollars to various charitable causes around the world.

Why the Reluctance Then?

The benefits of owning a business are self-evident and well-documented. The successes of entrepreneurs, even within local communities, are testaments to its potential in massively redirecting the course of our lives.Despite these benefits, there is a reluctance by many people to venture into entrepreneurship or business ownership.

a. Risks

Risks are one of the primary drivers of this reluctance towards starting and owning a business. Owning a business comes with risks and liability that many people find it as an unattractive option for growing their wealth base. Pursuing an entrepreneurial dream comes with financial risks. You stand to lose significant amount of money if the business fails. For some, a business venture may sink with their life savings or even a loan. This can be especially devastating if you are retired, and you put all your life savings in a business, and you don't realize a return on investment. Even when the business takes longer than expected to break even, you may struggle financially. Financial setbacks are usually hard to overcome. It may take years to recover from such a loss. This is why many people in secure jobs are reluctant to put their hard earned money into a business.

Other than financial risks, starting your own business also comes with product liability risk. The news is always inundated with stories of companies being sued and fined millions of dollars due to health and safety issues associated with their products. Such cases not only damage the reputation of a business but also cost millions of dollars in litigations. You are even more likely to end up in jail. Individuals who are at risk-averse always find business ownership too risky. They rarely venture out of the comfort zone offered by a secure job. Product liability is also tied to regulatory requirements. Any breach of these regulations carries a potential financial implication and even jail time in some cases.

Additionally, individuals who are risk-averse also find the risk of employee disagreements unattractive. A workplace can be a melting pot of diversity, which can easily lead to conflicts and disagreements among employees. As a business owner, you are directly responsible for handling such disagreements, which can sometimes be draining. Owning a business requires acquisition and development of effective conflict resolution skills, strategic management and interpersonal communication skills that would not be necessarily required in a secured job. Moreover, a business owner is vicariously responsible for the actions of their employees. As such, responsibility of any legal or illegal actions taken by an employee in the name of the business is transferable to the business and/or its owner. Many people would reluctantly agree to enter into a deal with such significant responsibilities, risks, and liabilities even if it comes with significant financial rewards.

However, risk aversion creates a sense of timidity that limits human potential. The history of mankind would have been too different if inventors and pioneers of revolutionary ideas did not bring their inventions to fruition because they were reluctant to take risks. Risks offer opportunities to think creatively and generate ideas that can minimize the liabilities and risks involved in any business idea. Successful pursuance of an entrepreneurial dream is not the product of risk and liability elimination. Rather, it is the ability of the entrepreneur to structure those risks in a manner that minimizes them or their effects. This is because risks and liabilities are ever present; you can't eliminate them completely.

b. Financial commitment and uncertainties

Many people, though informed of the benefits, are reluctant to venture into business ownership because of the accompanying financial commitment. The size of the venture notwithstanding, a business requires significant financial layout to successfully launch and run before it breaks even. Even with planning, there are hiccups that may delay the breaking even, which translates into a delayed return on investment. More discouraging is for many people is how to source for the starting capital. For many, the only feasible option may be our personal savings. Others may source from their retirement funds. Those who have investments may also opt to use their investments to start a business. A bank loan is also a viable option for some people so long as they have personal assets to use as collateral.

Either way, none of these options inspires a high sense of confidence. You'll be essentially withdrawing a well secured fund and pumping into a project with a certain level of uncertainty. Such funds will henceforth be unavailable for personal use. No family needs can be met using the funds. Few people are comfortable with the prospect of living in a family home that has been tied as collateral for a loan. It rarely gives a sense of comfort to many and especially those who are risk-averse. The stories of possession and auction by financial institutions to recover loans don't inspire a sense of confidence in many people either.

Whether in a secured job or an entrepreneur, the corporate landscape, and life in general, is marked by uncertainties. However, when you are a business owner the effects of uncertainties in the business world can be debilitating. Business is subjected to external factors that are beyond the control of the entrepreneur or the business. An economic downturn can easily cutback on the gains your business has achieved. A shift away from the demand projections you made at the onset of the business can have you scrambling back to the drawing board to save your business from going under. If your business is founded on a red ocean strategy, a seemingly simple act such as entrance of a new competitor can have ripple effects in the market that easily push you out of business. This is because a red ocean is characterized by cutthroat competition for a limited demand. Therefore, a new entrant changes the market dynamics especially when it comes to supply and demand.

c. *Susceptibility to a threat from external factors*

External factors fuel reluctance towards business ownership because they can easily stall the growth of an already established business. Moreover, it is difficult to anticipate them. Even the best simulation software and computer programs rarely get it right in projecting their occurrence. And the thought that you are committing your house's equity, retirement funds or savings to such a venture with uncertainties is discomforting. Many people prefer a high sense of surety, especially when it comes to money matters. While comprehensive planning can't take into account all these potential changes, strategic thinking can help an entrepreneur reinvent their strategies to take advantage of these situations.

d. *Lack of self-discipline*

There is a cause-effect relationship between self-discipline and success as an entrepreneur. Individuals who lack self-discipline or control lack the inner power and strength to hang on. Perseverance is a sign of inner fortitude. As a business owner, you need an almost superhuman level of confidence. Mastering your inner strength and self-control is critical when it comes to decision making and overall management of a business. Many business ideas and establishments have died premature deaths because the founders lacked the courage and patience to follow through on their plans. A small bump on the way and an entrepreneur with no self-discipline folds up the business. Persistence is a valuable quality that has transformed many start-ups into multibillion-dollar global entities.

The late Steve Jobs, the co-founder of Apple, is a classic example of persistence born out of self-discipline. When he pushed out of the company in 1985 due an escalation in power struggles, Jobs reinvented himself and founded new entities. These new ventures became so successful that Apple Inc. bought them and soon Steve Jobs was back at the helm of Apple. While away from Apple, he was patient enough. He had the self-discipline to reinvent himself, and when he came back to Apple, he revived the company and set on the path to revolutionary success it enjoys today. For his efforts, Steve Jobs is remembered as a pioneer of micro-computing technology and suave and charismatic entrepreneur and corporate leader. The importance of self-discipline as an entrepreneurial skill is not only exemplified in Steve Jobs' story; many multinational corporations such as Microsoft followed the same script: self-disciplined founders and leaders who were patient enough to follow through with the plans to make the business succeed.

Many people are reluctant to venture into entrepreneurship because they lack the self-discipline to continue pushing on in the face of setbacks and failures. And many more give business ownership a wide berth because they lack the patience to continue searching for strategic business ideas. They would rather settle for red ocean strategies where demand is the primary basis for competition. A red ocean is full of sharks and too many uncertainties. Competing for existing demand may seem like an obvious and easy choice for business strategy. But it is too risky. Uncertainties are abounded with such a strategy. In most cases, it is unsustainable because demand tends to reach its saturation point.

Truly self-disciplined entrepreneurs have the patience to come up with revolutionary ideas; ideas that allow them to operate in the blue ocean. Instead of fighting for demand in the red ocean, such entrepreneurs create demand. It is strategic thinking that requires patience and an inner strength that many people lack. A blue ocean strategy is a product of self-discipline. While many commentators readily quote the successes of the Canadian based circus company Cirque du Soleil as the epitome of blue ocean strategy and self-discipline, multinationals such as Microsoft, Amazon, and Apple can also be included in the list. Blue ocean strategy is the driver of success in the startup world. It is a product of self-discipline, a quality that many lacks. And it is a dearth that has seen many people feel reluctant to venture into business ownership. They lack the patience to commit time and money into a business idea that may break even after months or even a year. Their short perseverance span cannot accommodate the liabilities, risks, and uncertainties associated with owning a business despite knowing the potential benefits.

The Psychology and Science of Self-Discipline

If self-discipline is one of the pillars of success in life, that the question is, what does it mean? What does it entail? What are the psychological and scientific underpinnings of self-discipline? Self-disciple is the will power to exercise effortful restraint. It is the willpower to inhibit our impulses especially those with negative impacts on our overall well-being. An essential skill for all aspects of life, self-discipline is an inner strength. It is self-control. An individual with self-discipline has greater capacity to control their reactions to issues and situations. They have the inner strength to control their actions. The overall control of one's self is the product of self-discipline. When mastered and strengthened, self-discipline elevates our drive to follow through with our decisions. We are better placed to achieve our life goals, professional, and individual when we have the willpower and inner strength to stick to them in the face of challenges and difficulties.

However, inhabiting our impulses, especially those negative ones should not be misconstrued as being mean to yourself. It is a common misconception that individuals who are self-disciplined live a dull, restricted live shorn any fun and joys that come with life. Having self-discipline has nothing to do with being harsh to one's life. It does not compare in any way to living a limited life devoid of personal fulfillment.The essence of self-discipline is having the mental fortitude to persevere. When you persevere, you stand a better chance of accomplishing your goals than falling to the temptations of human indulgences. As a life skill, self-discipline is one of the primary keys to unlocking your inner strength to keep laziness and procrastination at bay. Following through with your aspirations and goals is important when it comes to beating unhealthy addictions.

A relentless pursuit of disciplined existence is hinged on delaying instant self-gratification for more wholesome, satisfying and greater benefits. It is both cognitive and psychological. As a cognitive ability, self-discipline allows an individual to delay gratification. As a thinking system, self-discipline defines our decision-making process. When we are more controlled, we tend to be more critical and objective in our analysis of situations before making decisions. Therefore, the final decisions we make are born out of knowledge, which is the essence of cognitive thinking.

Knowledgeable thinking system is based on four fundamentals elements:

Sensations: Sensations are mental pictures created through stimulation from the external environment. Self-disciplined individuals make decisions after visualizing their various outcomes. By mentally visualizing the outcomes of your decisions, you stand a better chance of making productive and effective decisions. Sensations are products of mental simulations.

Feelings: Feelings are internal sensitivities or perceptions of events and issues. When embraced in decision making, feelings can be powerful weapons that give us the inner strength to soldier on in the face of challenges. It gives us an elevated sense of ownership of our decisions.

Actions: Actions give a sense of practicality to the decisions you make. It ensures that you stay in touch with reality even as you make decisions. A self-disciplined individual deduces the practicality of hypothetical situations and makes decisions based on the outcome of such reflections.

Goals: These act as beacons for directing our steps. Goals are markers that guide us towards success. Self-discipline is the measure of how well we see through the plans we have to achieve our goals. Goals inspire action and shape our feelings.

Therefore, self-discipline, as a cognitive thinking system, ensures that the decisions we make are based on wholesome considerations. It combines both emotions, facts, and reality. We are then guided by both facts or realities and our feelings and sensations. As an aspiring business owner, self-discipline will ensure that you make the conscious decision persevere, not only because of your emotions. Your willpower will be driven by the goals you set and the practicality of your options. These elements will always remind you why it is important to delay gratification.

The elements – feelings, actions, goals, and sensations –allows for reflective analysis of situations. They help us in reigning in our reflexive human desire for instant gratification. The quest for instant gratification is a manifestation of a lack of perseverance. It shows that we are more inclined towards making impulsive decisions. As a business owner, a change in the economic forecast, entry of a new competitor, or financial hiccup can trigger impulsive decisions. Top in the list of actions that many business owners who lack self-discipline may take is closure of business. Sometimes this may seem like the viable option.

However, success in any sphere of life, and especially in business, has never been a straight line. As a business owner, you are bound to be hit by several curveballs. Your business plan and projections may be disrupted and thrown into disarray by a change in government policy or the entry of a new competitor. But, if the history of successful companies and individuals is anything to go by, then there is need for mental steeliness and perseverance.

The triggering of impulsive actions is innate. Adrenaline, the hormone that is responsible for determining how animals react to situations, is imprinted in the DNA. The choice to act impulsively is as a result of the brain triggering the flight mode. As a business owner, when the profit projections don't inspire confidence in the future success of the business, folding up is an impulsive action. If you feel threatened by a new competitor, closing shop may seem a viable course of action.

But these impulsive decisions are reflexive – not reflective. They are born out distractions and frustrations. When you are self-disciplined, you'll have the self-control and appeal to your sense of reason. You will explore the available options in spite of the frustrations and challenges. You'll decisions despite these challenges and not because of them. When the brain triggers the fight mode, you follow through your plans; you fight on. The use your feelings, goals, and sensations to spur you into action. And this is the path that successful business entities and entrepreneurs take almost on a daily basis.

Psychologically, an individual must devise strategies to steer their mind clear of the temptation to settle for short term benefits. Resisting urges for a greater benefit calls for mentally conditioning yourself through different strategies. You have to make the conscious decision to embark on such a journey. You must consciously invest your emotions and cognitive abilities to be self-discipline. Self-discipline is not an instantaneous achievement; achieving it requires building from strength to strength.

Importance of Self-Discipline in Business

Pursuing a life of disciplined existing and inhibiting our impulses come several benefits as discussed below:

a. Character building

Self-determination is highly valued in many liberal societies, including the United States where the concept is entrenched in the constitution as a fundamental right. At the core of self-determination is character. You are at liberty to build your character using life experiences and teachings as the building blocks. Self-discipline helps in building inner strength and a habit of perseverance and positive outlook of life. Having a positive outlook on life and resilience even in the face of challenges and frustrations of life is critical for social and professional interactions. It is a healthy habit that can build you. By mastery self-control, you set yourself on a path to success.

Sometimes it is not enough to be caring and philanthropic, yet you have impulsive. You can easily implode under the weight of frustrations or hot temper. Then your caring nature gets lost in the maze of emotions and impulsivity. A highly skilled and talented individual will struggle to succeed in any work environment if they lack self-discipline. They are less likely to beat the urges of procrastination and laziness. Others may battle addictions and short temper. Many employers would be unwilling to hire or retain such an individual. Your social circle may thin out if you lack self-control to persevere in any relationship.

As a business owner, self-discipline is a habit to cultivate. To succeed, you will need to be consistent and work hard towards your goals. Success in the business world comes to those who remain committed to their organizational goals and develop strategies to overcome challenges without losing sight of the goals. It is a labor of love that can only be achieved through developing a high sense of inner strength and willpower. You'll be better place to handle workplace issues such as employee conflicts better when you have inculcated a healthy habit of self-control.

Self-determination is not confined to humans. The concept is transferable to businesses. Branding in business is the product of self0-determination. As a business owner, you must consistently work on your business brand and position it strategically in the marketplace. It is an arduous task and no mean fete. It requires time and resources, both financial and cognitive, to achieve. Self-discipline is the glue that holds these ingredients together.

b. Boosting your focus and work ethics

Developing a healthy work ethic can easily set you apart, even in a crowded workplace. You are more likely to accomplish tasks and achieve set goals when you have a positive work ethic. A positive work ethic is a manifestation of self-discipline. Such an individual is cognizant of the challenges and difficulties associated with completing tasks. However, they have the discipline to rise above these challenges. They challenge themselves every day to accomplish tasks because they are inspired and driven by the need to achieve set goals and objectives. Hence, they persevere and draw from inner strength to accomplish tasks. Disciplined individuals stick to the course set from the onset.

The focus of a self-disciplined individual is laser-sharp because they have mastered the art of focusing on the bigger picture in spite of the distractions. They train their minds to pursue the singular goal of succeeding or accomplishing a goal. A boosted focus and work ethics are important ingredients for individual and professional growth and development.

The benefits of work ethics and sharp focus for an entrepreneur are manifold. Worth ethics is critical in avoiding the urges of procrastination and laziness, which are commonplace in self-employment. Self-employment creates a false sense of job security, which can easily lead to procrastination and laziness. You stand to lose vital contacts, contracts, and even manpower if you are a lazy entrepreneur who likes to procrastinate. Laziness and procrastination translate to lateness in delivering projects, making payments to employees and attending to vital business engagements such as meetings. With focus and good work ethics, you can keep these vices at bay and steer your company towards operational and financial success.

c. *Mastery of new skills*

Possession of multiple gives a professional versatility that is undeniably attractive for headhunters and employers. Multi-skilled individuals are proficient at task completion and serve in different roles in different situations within the work environment. Such individuals also find it easier to grow other aspects of their lives, such as building and maintaining social relations. However, mastering new skills calls for having a relentless spirit, a determination founded on self0-discipline.

For an entrepreneur, having multiple skills can be the difference between breaking even and closing shop in the first month of operation. When you found a business, chances that you will be the primary decision maker are high. Most of the managerial duties, responsibilities, and issues will land on your desk on a daily basis. Whether through short courses or experience, learn different skills. But mastery of any skill requires perseverance. Therefore, you need self-discipline to persevere in business challenges. It will also come in handy when you choose to improve your decision making ability through skill mastery.

d. Achieving success

Improved focus, skill mastery, focus, and habit development all converged towards driving your success agenda forward. The true essence and most evident benefit of self-discipline are helping you get things done and succeeding while at it. When your focus is laser sharp and have a positive work ethic, you are more likely to succeed in anything you set out to do. If you have built a positive character and habit through self-discipline, you can put the multiple skills you have acquired into good use and succeed. While these assertions are not cast on stone, it is indisputable that self-discipline significantly increases your chances of success.

Self-discipline strengthens your mental fortitude. It creates a winning mentality and gives you self-esteem and confidence to face situations with motivation and confidence. Your drive to accomplish tasks and achieve the desired goals becomes heightened with self-control. You develop a 'success' mentality. You become a master of pursuing your goals. Success is a product of mastery. As you become a master of positive and winning mentality, so is your personal growth and development. Mastery, on the other hand, comes through self-discipline.

As a business owner, challenges are abound. Obstacles and barriers to the success of your business venture may come in different forms and sizes. From personal limitations to internal and external business environment, the corporate sector is full of highs and lows. However, when you are disciplined, goal achievement and persistence become healthy habits. When preserve and persist when faced with the frustrations, distractions, and challenges of life and business management, you will taste the glory that many disciplined entrepreneurs have enjoyed since time immemorial.Perseverance and persistence turns dreams into reality. Self-discipline is the key to building lasting relationships with stakeholders including employees, investors, customers and business partners.

If self-discipline is an important piece in the 'success jigsaw puzzle,' then why does it seem that many people are deficient in this vital life skill? The problem is how self-discipline is mastered. An individual must devise strategies to steer their mind clear of the temptation to settle for short term benefits. Resisting urges for greater benefit calls for mentally conditioning yourself through different strategies. You have to make the conscious decision to embark on such a journey. You must consciously invest your emotions and cognitive abilities to be self-discipline. Self-discipline is not an instantaneous achievement; achieving it requires building from strength to strength. Making such investments is difficult. On the face value, strengthening your willpower and mastering it requires consistency to purpose. You've to constantly train your mind and master how to control your impulses.

VISION
MISSION
VALUES

CHAPTER 2: The Power of Self-discipline

To be successful in business, you need to focus on your personality, rather than material things or your job. In this chapter, you will acquire various tips on how to master and utilize self-discipline to become the person you have always wanted to be. Moreover, you will learn the art of developing more exceptional personal pride, self-esteem, and self-respect. You will see how to create crucial disciplines essential for building a strong persona.

Furthermore, you will learn how to incorporate them into your personality and character. Self-discipline is not natural, but those who follow it can see life more positively and achieve success in the long run. Despite many people knowing self-discipline, the majority still fail in their lives and undertakings. No one likes living on a set of restrictions and rules, and this pretty much presents a challenge to those who wish to live a life of discipline.

Why is self-discipline hard to foster?

Self-discipline is not a matter of limiting yourself to a set of rules. Contrary to popular belief, self-restraint allows you to live the life you truly desire. As a habit that is mastered through learning, self-discipline requires daily practice. Habits dictate the type of relationship between your wants and the surrounding. Self-discipline requires you to alter your habits and the surrounding. You start seeing things in a different light. It is a complete overhaul of who you were. Self-discipline requires commitment and sacrifice.

As humans, we can choose between right and wrong. Discipline yourself to do things in the right way and at the right time. If you have a strong will, you can adhere to set rules, and you will lead a good life. Otherwise, your life will never have any meaning. Self-discipline gives you full control of your life, despite past failures.

Importance of self-discipline

Self-discipline is a resourceful inner power that gives us the ability to continue fighting and not loses hope, despite the endless setbacks and failures. A self-disciplined person possesses self-control, and the will to ward off distractions and temptations that keep us from fulfilling goals in life. Self-discipline forms the basis by which stable and real success are achieved.

Life tends to throw challenges our way, and it can be difficult dealing with all of them. To overcome hurdles and challenges, it is crucial to have the self-discipline to enable us to face the challenges and overcome them. Possessing this restraint also allows us to remain healthy and generate positive energy.

Restrain boosts character and makes life more meaningful. Understanding the importance of self-discipline and practicing it helps you to have a controllable experience. Moreover, it brings out the inner strength, beat addictions, and overcome procrastination and laziness. It provides you with the ultimate gratification, pleasure, and overall happiness. Acquiring self-discipline is difficult at first, but practice makes it easier.

Besides, your will to persevere, resist temptations, and the potential to win will double. Self-discipline plays a crucial role in treating addictions and eating disorders. The importance of self-discipline cannot be ignored. Self -discipline gives us the ability to choose how we want to live our lives. It also helps us to get all that we want in life. Another added advantage of self-discipline is that it makes it easier to achieve dreams and ambitions.

The Key to Ultimate Happiness

Contrary to the idea that self-discipline deprives people of happiness and pleasures, studies by scholars prove the opposite. Recent research shows that self-disciplined people are happier both in the present and in the long term. People with self-control can avoid environments that could have the potential to stir problematic conflicts and desires. By doing so, they can stay away from numerous negative emotions. Many people think that self-disciplined people are annoying and have nothing to offer. However, such people live authentic and fulfilled lives. An example can be food and health. Disciplined individuals avoid environments where junk food is likely to be served to lower the risk of falling victim to desires and feeling bad about it.

When we are successful, we are happy. Being disciplined makes us successful. To achieve discipline, the desire has to come from within and cannot be forced. The earlier we start forging discipline in our lives, the better it is to adapt it into our daily routines. You cannot become disciplined overnight. It takes time and needs patience.

Ten Reasons Why Self-Discipline Is Imperative to Success

A disciplined business person is patient, can visualize his grand plan, and stay on course. He trusts his endeavors and believes he can achieve more through perseverance and determination. Self-discipline helps you make the right decisions. You take your time before making decisions. Moreover, when you are self-disciplined, you know when to act and when to restrain.

Being disciplined is the ultimate way to become successful. You cannot go without it. Successful people always outline self-discipline as one of the tenets of success. However, the big question is, why is self-discipline crucial for one to succeed? Self-discipline provides you with inner energy to propel you to the most magnificent peaks in life. Start training yourself to become discipline if you want to accomplish it. There will be times when the only discipline can save you. Below are ten reasons why self-discipline is vital for success.

1. Boosts inner strength

Self-control gives confidence and inner strength, which enables you to make choices in a relaxed way. In a self-disciplined work environment, workers can control responses and actions in a positive manner.

2. Provides the willpower to adhere to your commitments

A self-disciplined manager is what companies want. Managing difficult situations becomes easy when you are disciplined. It enables you to change adverse conditions into good ones and improves employee relations. Many business people agree that self-discipline helped them to adhere to their rules, regardless of the circumstance.

3. Upgrades your approach

A disciplined entrepreneur can think beyond the breaking points. With a reasonable objective and strategy, entrepreneurs can enhance their working system and improve their attitude towards their overall goal. Furthermore, it gets rid of procrastination, laziness, and addictions. Self-discipline makes entrepreneurs passionate and inventive towards their business.

4. Makes you an implementer

The significance of business and life is created among entrepreneurs through discipline. It creates a way to adhere to resolutions, even the hectic ones. It also gives you visions and informs you on how to gauge your prosperity. Many entrepreneurs concur that discipline encourages them to create blueprints of their plans, expanding the trust and conviction among themselves and the employees.

5. Self-control makes a propensity

Habits can make or destroy you. Self-Discipline builds habits in life that develop through discipline. The vast majority of people lack control in their lives primarily because of laziness. They need to realize that procrastination is a habit, and it can be changed. Successful individuals teach themselves to work and remain consistent through discipline until it becomes a habit. They succeed because of self-discipline.

6. It encourages you to complete things

Self-discipline is critical to getting things done. It can be anything. Through self-discipline, you can resolve to read inspirational books or complete an errand within a given timeline. If you train yourself to complete each and everything, you create a character around it. This routine gives you success in life. Self-discipline is significant for progress. It encourages you to be reliable throughout everyday life, and when you are steady, you will accomplish anything you need.

7. It makes you focused

We live in a world full of interruptions. Self-discipline causes you to concentrate on your objectives. Moreover, it encourages you to adhere to the work you need to complete to make progress. When you are focused on your goals, you will finish each and everything that needs your attention. Productive individuals have a strong focus. They focus on the objectives and accomplishments of life whenever possible. This, in turn, propels them to higher levels of achievement. A disciplined person is not easily distracted. He/she knows what is at stake and gives it their full attention.

8. It boosts self-confidence

Success goes to the person who has faith in him/herself and works hard. Having good ideas is not enough to succeed. You must put those ideas into action, which requires discipline. Self-discipline encourages you to have work ethics. Moreover, it boosts your confidence. If you teach yourself to be disciplined, you improve your hard-work ethics by adhering to it. It will help you achieve your goals. Your self-esteem rises when you achieve goals set for the day. It is not a must that you succeed in many areas. You gain the zeal to continue when you appreciate yourself for little achievements. It makes you the best in your area of expertise.

9 Disciplined people are the ones who succeed, not complacent ones.

One way of succeeding at what you do is to improve on areas of weaknesses. Doing this boosts your confidence and makes you a better person or employee. You become an expert by working hard and spending at least 10,000 hours to learn a craft. Discipline goes hand in hand with mastery. Many people fail in their endeavors because they don't try hard enough to achieve mastery. Successful individuals focus on only one task/craft until they become masters in the task. It is through this form of dedication and perseverance that self-discipline will usher in mastery, which breeds success.

10. It makes you the best version of yourself.

Success is possible for only those who work hard. You cannot succeed without qualities such as discipline, hard work, and commitment. You need to improve every day. You need to be the best you can be to end up successful throughout everyday life. Self-discipline leads to individual improvement and enables you to actualize your dreams. When you accomplish something, you become a better version of yourself every day. Self-control is significant for progress and development in life.

To sum it up...

Self-discipline plays a crucial role in achieving success. Instead of complaining every day, do something about your situation. As they say, practice makes perfect. Train yourself every day, and it is only a matter of time before you become self-disciplined. No human is limited, and everyone has the potential to achieve anything they desire in life. All that is needed is self-discipline. Instead of idling around, start working on tasks that will push you closer to your goals.

Ten incredible ways to master self-discipline

Like everything else in life that spurs progress, extreme struggles we face are within us. It is for this reason that learning self-discipline is essential. A person with a high level of restraint spends less energy deliberating whether to enjoy habits that are unfavorable to their well-being and can settle on positive choices. They don't give in to impulses or give sentiments a chance to direct their decisions. Instead, they settle on practical arrangements. By doing this, they increase the chances of feeling happiness. As an individual, there are things you can do to master self-restraint and increase the resolution to have a joyful life. Below are ten things you can do to acquire self-discipline.

1. Identify your shortcomings

Every individual has his or her weaknesses. Whether it is snacking on chocolate chip treats or potato chips, or making bad decisions, we all have our pitfalls. Shortcomings can be the pathway to success if we understand and work on them. The first step is to take advantage of your strongholds and work on areas of weaknesses. Don't be embarrassed about your shortcomings. Embrace them, and wonders will happen.

Recognize your weaknesses. Many people ignore their shortcomings and pretend that they don’t exist. However, ignoring your weaknesses is wrong because it prevents you from becoming the best version of yourself. Accept all your flaws.

2. *Avoid temptations*

The adage out of sight out of mind is an expression that may appear silly but offers incredible counsel. By expelling your most significant enticements from your reach, you will improve your self-restraint. If you want to a healthy lifestyle, refrain from buying junk food. It is as simple as that. If places you frequent are full of junk, go elsewhere.

Moreover, if you want to improve your efficiency at work, disable notification alerts and put your mobile phone in vibration or silent mode. The fewer interruptions you have, the more you will focus on your work. Set yourself up for a better life by discarding negative influences.

3. *Set clear objectives and have an execution plan*

Set clear goals to guide you on what to do next. You should likewise have a comprehension of what achievement intends to you. It is easy to lose focus if you don't lay down what you want to achieve. Moreover, create an execution plan to make work easy. Describe the execution plan in detail to avoid confusion.

A reasonable plan details every progress you make to arrive at the objectives. Make a mantra to keep yourself focused on the goals. Successful people set clear goals and stick to them. It helps them to remain on track.

4. Work on your self-discipline

No one is born with disciplined. It is a learned behavior. Therefore, it needs regular practice and dedication. For you to succeed at anything, discipline is at the forefront. It will keep you in line when you faced with challenges. It will prevent you from giving up on your dreams because of difficulties. Similar to going to the gym, self-discipline, and willpower take a great deal of effort. The focus and work that self-discipline needs can be depleting. Over the long haul, it can turn out to be harder to hold your resolution under control. Build your self-discipline through day by day steadiness. Set resolutions and stick to them. Maintain a positive attitude when faced with challenges.

5. Make new routines by keeping it straightforward

Having self-restraint and creating a new habit can be overwhelming during the first stages, mainly if you give the task at hand priority. Keep it straightforward to avoid feeling defeated. Break your objectives into little, feasible steps. Rather than attempting to make a big difference without rest, focus on accomplishing one thing reliably and ace self-discipline in light of that objective.

If you want to get fit, start by hitting the gym for 10 or 15 minutes every day. In case you are trying to improve your sleep pattern, start by getting in bed 15 minutes sooner every night. Also, if you need to eat more nutritious foods, begin by preparing lunch the previous night to take with you the following day. Make child strides. In the long run, when you're ready, you can add more objectives to the list of your goals.

6. Eat healthily and frequently

The sentiment of being hungry - that furious, irritated, disturbed sensation you get when you're experiencing hunger pangs is genuine and can affect willpower. It has been proven that low blood sugar debilitates an individual's determination, making you pessimistic and cantankerous.

You cannot think properly when you are hungry. Your focus is impaired when you don't take care of yourself.

The first step toward regaining control of your life has a healthy lifestyle. Other areas of your life are affected when you neglect one aspect. Have regular meals and healthy bites to keep you in check.

7. Change your idea about determination

Research shows that the level of self-control and individual has dictated by their convictions. If you don't work hard to fix your areas of weakness, it is impossible to be confident. Get rid of things that threaten your confidence. Self-discipline is an important attribute that cannot be overlooked. It has the potential to change anyone from a failure to a victor. What matters is your commitment to change. You must be willing to eliminate bad behaviors to attain self-discipline. Our inside conceptions determine how much self-control and willpower we have. You can actualize anything you put your mind. What hinders many from restraining themselves is giving up too early. Becoming self-discipline is a journey that takes time. The good this is that it can be acquired over time.

8. Give yourself a reinforcement plan

Psychology experts use an implementation intention procedure to understand willpower. It is essential to formulate a plan to manage a troublesome circumstance you realize you will probably confront. For example, if you want to embark on a healthy lifestyle journey, motivate yourself to stay on course. There will be days when you will not have the momentum. Remind yourself why you started in the first place. Perseverance leads to self-discipline. Before attending a party, convince yourself that as opposed to eating a plate of crackers and cheese, you will have a glass of water and mingle with other people at the party. Going in with a backup will assist you to have the attitude for the occasion. Furthermore, you will spare your energy by not settling on an abrupt choice dependent on your emotional state.

9. Reward yourself

Reward yourself with something beautiful every time you achieve your objectives. This will motivate you to work harder. Similar to how a little child gets a treat for ethical conduct, reward yourself when you succeed. The expectation is amazing. It gives you something to focus on, so you are not worried about what you have not achieved. Also, when you accomplish your objective, set another target and a new reward to keep yourself pushing forward.

10. Forgive yourself and move on

You cannot win all the time. Even with the best goals and well-laid plans, sometimes we miss the mark. You will have good and bad times, triumphs, and inauspicious disappointments. The secret is to continue pushing ahead. In case of a stumble, pick yourself up and try again. Don't give up when you fail the first time. Try not to give yourself a chance to get enveloped with blame, outrage, or dissatisfaction. Getting emotional will drag you further down and obstruct future advancement. Learn from your failures and move on. Successful people tried many times before they had their first breaks.

What you want and how to get it

If you can reflect on your life right now, what you say about it? Are you successful? And if the answer is no, why is that the case? Why have you not achieved success and happiness at the moment?

Apart from the various reasons, there is one basic answer that can explain the situation: you have not mastered the concept of self-discipline. You do not do the necessary things that can help you in achieving the success you so desire. Looking at this logically, what would it take for you to achieve success in all aspects of your life?

Odds are, it is a well-known fact. Everyone knows what is needed to get fit, yet the number of people that are fit is minimal. Most employees understand what is required to better their performance at work, yet very few individuals are eager to do it. Everybody knows which foods are beneficial and which ones to stay away from. However, many individuals will still choose to snack on chocolate chip biscuits instead of veggies, fruits, and raw food.

In other words, all the knowledge acquired so far is not useful enough if you do not have the necessary habits that enhance your self-discipline to utilize the information at your disposal for your betterment. Elbert Hubbard talks about self-discipline as "the capacity to do what should be done, when the need arises, regardless of whether you feel like doing it or not." It is the fundamental skill required to prevail in any undertaking. A successful life originates from the consistent choices you make regularly— and only through self-discipline are we able to do that.

Therefore, it is essential to devise and implement a way in which self-discipline can be acquired, sustained, and improved. The basics involve starting from scratch, building the concept little by little over time, and maintaining consistency.

Ways of Attaining Unbeatable Self-Discipline

If it is to be it is up to me

Regardless of what objectives and goals you set throughout your life, there is one incredible law that determines the outcome of what you do: only you can ascend the ladder of success. Nobody else is liable for your well-being, riches, progress, or bliss. Whatever happens to you is a result of your efforts, hard work, resource investments, and above all, the right mindset. This means you are answerable to yourself and are responsible for the decisions you make.

You get to choose the job that will pay the bills, the individuals you live with, and how much you wish to exercise each day. You decide how you spend your time, and the choices you make consistently will reveal the moment of truth to your life as you go by.

If you desire a successful life, you will have to settle on better choices. You can reprimand other individuals for the lack of happiness or results in your life. However, much of this doesn't transform anything. Your transformation, growth, development, and improvements are solely in your hands. They depend on what you do, how you do it, and above all, why. Assume the responsibility for the aspect of your life, regardless of whether or not you can directly influence them. This ten-word phrase is an essential affirmation that should give you a sense of direction and reminder when you deviate from the course.

Avoid the enemies of success

Brian Tracy - a renowned motivational speaker, is quoted saying, "the greatest foe to any success is the path of least resistance." When you decide to do what is fun and straightforward over what is essential, you will never attain the happiness and degrees of accomplishment that you desire. That is because each extraordinary triumph requires incredible sacrifice. If being successful was simple, everyone would be successful. But since the victory in life has a cost and requires diligent work, many people will never arrive at their maximum potential.

If you decide to procrastinate on the essential things, you not only waste your chance to develop as an individual but also lose trust in yourself. You begin to consider yourself to be sluggish and ineffective, and that mental self-portrait will turn into a successful prophecy. For whatever the mind thinks, the body does.

There are three basic requirements to accomplish any set objective. The first is having a distinctive vision for what you need. This can also be referred to as a sense of purpose or intent. Secondly, you have to forge a strategy for getting where you want to be. Prior planning gives a guideline or steps that can be followed to achieve success. This is one of the most fundamental elements of self-discipline. Last but not least, all plans must be implemented for the goal to be completed. This calls for consistent actions and efforts towards the objective.

While the initial two sections make the unaffected parts of the equation, many individuals battle with the last part, which is hard work. There is nothing that you can't accomplish with diligent practice, so you must foster the habit of doing what is difficult and fundamental over what is fun and straightforward. Doing this is likely the surest method to prevail throughout everyday life.

Focusing Ahead

According to Abraham Lincoln, "The ideal approach to anticipate the future is to create it." If you want to know where you will be in the next five years, take a close inspection of your life now. You have to identify the necessary steps you are currently making to help you turn your objectives into reality.

Many people tend to think that their lives will abruptly change for the better, but very few practically put an effort to influence the change. If you are not content with your present conditions, would you say you are doing what is necessary to transform them? If not, you are merely wandering off in the land of fantasy. Change comes where there is action.

We are what we repeatedly do. Success then isn't a demonstration, but a habit (Aristotle). An incredible method to effectively create your future is to question yourself. If I already accomplished my life goals, what books would I read? How would I behave? How frequently would I hit the gym, and what would I be doing in the office the whole day? When you answer these questions, you realize what to do. Go about your life as though you were already successful.

Obstacles are part of the journey

Throughout everyday life, nothing worth having comes on a silver platter. You need to make some sacrifices in the form of hard work, time, pain, and effort if, indeed, you wish to succeed. There will be numerous setbacks, and whenever you draw near to at long last succeeding, there will be some greater difficulty testing how much you genuinely want it. Solely in the wake of passing the first test, and after that another, will you have the option to succeed?

The biggest catastrophe of life is that many people lose hope right before they achieve success. They already made it five yards to the finish line, and all they need is one last push to complete the race and bring home the sweet triumph. In most cases, just before they do that, there is one previous impediment blocking their way — one final disappointment that they have to survive. Too many people surrender at that moment, without realizing how close they were.

If you are to take one thing from this chapter simply, let it be this: Whenever you experience disappointment and setbacks, continue pushing forward. That amount of self-discipline is enough to guide your success. Remember, if it was simple, anyone could do it. In any case, it's hard, and that is your opportunity to isolate yourself from the individuals that don't need success as badly as you do. The best way to develop as an individual is by confronting the most considerable difficulties throughout everyday life and enduring the suffering long enough to succeed. Regardless of the extent it takes or how hard it gets, convince yourself that it is never over until you win!

Rewrite Your Goals Every Day

To stay self-disciplined all through, you must remember the master goal; the long-term objective. Just by recollecting why you are doing whatever you are doing, you will take the necessary steps and follow through regardless of whether it gets hard. All things considered, you don't merely buckle down for reasons unknown. You have explicit goals that you need to accomplish, despite all the trouble. As Nietzsche stated, "He who has a "why" to live for can withstand practically any "how." I accept this to be totally valid. If you realize what you need to do and you have enough motivation to do it, you will take the necessary steps to achieve it.

Sometimes, we get so caught up working and accomplishing the goals that we overlook why we began in any case. We forget why we do what we do and somewhat get overpowered by a seemingly endless daily agenda. It is no big surprise that most people appear too subdued and even exhausted with life. They have no goals to work for.

The best approach to solve the problem is by rewriting your objectives every day and envisioning the future as you want it to be. Every time you wake up in the morning, jot down the most important goals you want to achieve in life. This will get you excited and motivated, and at the same time, make it completely clear on what you have to do to succeed. This is called the active setting of goals. When you stay focused on your vision for life and goals, you can settle on choices that add value to those goals.

Before Starting, Vow to Never Give Up

To ensure that you remain stable in the face of challenges, formulate beforehand how you would respond to the problems when they happen. Have a well laid out back up plan should things go sideways, or else it will be a matter of when you are going to give up. When jotting down your goals, focus on seeing them to fruition, regardless of how hard it might be.

Decide how you will react to setbacks and disappointments so you can bounce back more rejuvenated and focused than ever before. This approach, also called risk assessment is essential in mitigating possible impediments along the way. When you abide by this commitment and vow never breaks it, you will prevail at anything you set your focus on. The results may not be immediate, but they will be definite.

Keep away distractions

Abide by the well-known adage, "out of sight, out of mind." keep all distractions and allurements far from reach. This will be the very first step when striving to improve your self-control. If you wish to possess more control over your eating, avoid junk food. To enhance your concentration while working, turn off your smartphone, and keep your work area clean. If this doesn't work for you, download the Self-control application on your PC to block chat sites such as Facebook, or even video watching sites such as YouTube for a set timeframe. Set yourself up for affluence by discarding the distractions.

Eat healthily... and regularly

Studies have demonstrated that low blood sugar tends to soften a person's resolve. A hungry person cannot concentrate since his or her brain does not function optimally. Hunger makes it hard to focus on the job beforehand, not to mention the grumpiness and pessimistic feelings.

In this state, you are more prone to have a tired feeling of restraint in all aspects of your life - diet, work out, relationships, work, and so on. To remain on track, ensure that you stay full throughout the day by having meals and snacks every few hours. You can choose to have some muscle milk or almonds around. With these two, you are guaranteed some fats and proteins anytime you need them during the day.

Eating frequently keeps your glucose levels in check and improves your focus and ability to make decisions. Permit your mind to concentrate on more pressing issues such as your goals rather than on your snarling stomach.

It is ever the right moment-start now

Fostering your self-restraint means interfering with your usual routine, which can be awkward and unpleasant. A learned behavior repeated over time, becomes a habit. When a pattern is formed, the decision-making process is impaired, and you are forced to function as an automated device. At first, peeling off a bad habit will feel wrong, and the brain will do everything to resist the change. It is at this point that you should totally embrace the new switch and incorporate it into your standard regimen until the new habit becomes a norm. To foster the new practice, make effective decisions, and chug along until the habit becomes natural and pleasant.

Reward yourself to treats and breaks

Self-control doesn't mean your new routine should be complete without any relaxing moments or gifts. Truth be told, going entirely cold turkey often brings about disappointments, failures, and resorting to your old habits. While practicing self-discipline, include treats, rewards, and breaks for yourself.

Are you trying dieting? Choose Sunday as the only day you get an ice cream treat. Are you attempting to get more fit? Give yourself the relaxing treat at a massage parlor after intense physical exercise. Are you trying to control your spending? Permit yourself a $20 binge spend at the shopping mall on Saturday. (Carry cash only and leave the credit cards at home). Self-discipline is hard. Always reward your progress.

Pardon yourself and push forward

Changing your way of thinking or doing things won't always work out as expected. You will experience remarkable triumphs, flat out disappointments, and some ups and downs. The secret is to continue pushing forward. In the event of a setback, recognize the reasons behind the setback and carry on. Don't get enveloped with blame, frustration, or outrage. These negative emotions won't help with your self-discipline. Instead, utilize the setbacks as learning experiences for future endeavors. Pardon yourself, and get back on track immediately. The more you're off your game, the harder it is to stay focused on your goals.

Habits and fundamentals of self-discipline

Sleeping and self-discipline

Sleep is a physiological necessity that is hard to resist, no matter how much you would try. Sleep induces self-control through glucose levels. Enough sleep restores internal reserves of self-control and invariably controls plasticity in the brain, which aids in solidifying the learned habit. Better sleep ensures minimal psychological strain and improved self-control.

Benefits of good sleep

1. You develop better stable emotions

2. Learn skills faster
3. Build better muscles faster
4. Helps you to stay fit
5. How to utilize self-discipline to wake up consistently every day
6. Develop a habit of waking up the same time every day, let's say at 5 in the morning.
7. Build a habit of obeying the alarm clock when it rings. If you are likely to snooze it, keep it far away from the bed. That way, you will be forced to come out of bed to silence the alarm.

Nutrition

Do you ever feel bad about yourself after eating? You probably have bad eating habits. But lucky for you, there are ways to beat this bad habit as you will soon find out.

Tips to gain self-control over your life and get over food cravings

1. ***Learn how to counter stress***

Meditating twice a day can help improve your moods, return your cortisol levels to normal, and improve your well-being.

2. ***Incorporate mindfulness when eating***

Take a moment of thought before eating something. Find out if your body really needs what you are about to consume. Eat only when relaxed and do so slowly. Eating mindfully will help you get over food addictions and make you feel better when you are choosing foods that you wish to consume.

3. ***Check your blood sugar levels***

Food cravings are brought about by blood sugar imbalances. When you eat a balanced diet in the morning comprising of proteins, cholesterol-free fats, and vegetables, you are assured of stable blood sugar levels and smoother emotions.

4. Sleep well

Enough sleep guarantees reduced cortisol levels and less fatigue, which can lead to sugar cravings.

5. Stock your fridge with health-friendly foods

Out of sight, out of mind. Ensure that you keep only the healthy foods around and keep away temptations from yourself until you learn how to control your cravings and treat yourself only once in a while.

Exercise

Like any other thing that requires mastery, self-discipline can be learned, and to do so will require repetition and vigorous training every other day. When you learn to be disciplined, you will be more rational when you make decisions and have the power to overcome all manner of obstacles and achieve your goals even more quickly.

Below are some excellent and practical exercises you can utilize in your daily routine to improve your self-discipline.

1. Practice physical exercise daily. Regular exercise helps a great deal in improving your self-discipline. Exercise will boost your focus on tasks at hand. This way, you will learn how to fulfill your goals and persevere the process by which you achieve them.

2. Meditation. It is useful in improving fitness, mental well-being, and moods. To still your mind during meditation calls for effective self-control and is thus an excellent exercise for those who wish to master self-discipline.
3. Cold showers. Starting your day with a cold bath is a definite illustration of self-discipline. It is a simple habit that you can include in your daily routine.

Mindfulness

Mindfulness is a technique of using concentration in a particular sense to train focus and awareness of the situation. The practice is mostly aimed at achieving mental and emotional clarity and calm. Mediation can be aimed at reducing stress, enhancing personal well-being, realizing peace, and promoting perception. The essentials of this process are limitless.

CHAPTER 3: Mental Endurance

Positive thinking is an important building block for mental endurance, creativity, and life and work/business success.

Negativity can ruin self-discipline.

Mental endurance refers to stamina and toughness that empowers you to achieve the goals you set your eyes on in life – be it family, career, or spiritual. Watching sports, we have all admired athletes' fit bodies and the ability to run long miles. Behind that greatness is something most people overlook- mental endurance.

As an athlete, you must be in the right frame of mind. It is not enough to be in perfect shape or have many fans. You must have positive thoughts and believe that you can achieve your goal. Athletes reach their goals by cultivating positive thoughts. We can learn a lot from athletes and the importance of mental stamina. Granted, we all face several challenges in life. Some are minor and are dealt with instantly. However, others are complex and require mental endurance. You need mental stamina if your boss is demanding. You cannot last long in a stressful work environment without mental endurance. You will quit your job with hopes of finding a better one.

The truth is every job is demanding, and running a successful business is equally tough, more so in this competitive economy. You need mental endurance to make tough business decisions. The same way you need mental stamina when caring for elderly parents or teenagers. Many people think that mental endurance is being fruitful in anything that you do, regardless of the circumstances. People believe that when you can ignore your injuries, poor weather, and the pressure, then you have mental endurance. The truth is that you cannot produce good results consistently without mental endurance. No one is born with mental endurance. It is developed when one is exposed to challenging situations. When you go through tough times, you have no choice but to persevere. Self-discipline is essential in mental endurance.

Importance of Mental Endurance

- **Improves focus**- Mental endurance improves concentration. If you had a rough time understanding things, it becomes better when you endure. This is because your mind is clear and allows you to focus on present things.

- **Self-discipline**- you learn self-discipline from mental endurance. If you were the kind of person who liked instant gratification, you learn the value of waiting. Mental endurance teaches you patience, calmness, and self-control. You start valuing important things in life.

- **Leadership**- mental endurances can help you develop strong leadership skills that you will need for your business' success. It teaches you leadership qualities such as patience and perseverance. Moreover, it informs you that you have to wait for the good things in life.

Simple tips that can help you develop strong mental endurance

Many people are struggling with developing mental stamina. They believe that it is unattainable and resign to fate. The good news is that you can develop your mental stamina like athletes. You can challenge your mind to improve your mental endurance. There are brain exercises you can do, including crosswords, and solving puzzles. Such exercises require your mind to recall details. Video games are also great for challenging the brain to build mental endurance.

Health experts have emphasized the benefits of physical exercises for the longest time. Did you know that physical exercise is also good for the mind and brain? Exercise sends oxygen to the brain, which enables it to function properly. People are also advised to focus on what they are doing to improve focus and mental stamina. You are better off focusing on one activity at a time rather than taking on multiple activities simultaneously. You can move to another thing once you are done with one. Many people do not know this, but focusing on one thing is better than doing multiple things at once.

Follow the tips below to improve your mental endurance.

- **Change your attitude**- one thing that hinders many people from achieving their goals in life is bad. If you are the kind of person who does not see good in others or yourself, it will be difficult to improve your mental endurance. Instead of seeing the impossible, start believing it can be done. You cannot go anywhere with a bad attitude. It will hinder you from succeeding at anything you touch. Moreover, a bad attitude leads to more problems and prevents you from recognizing the problem at hand. Therefore, the first thing you need to do to improve your mental endurance is to change your attitude. You can do this by speaking positive affirmations every morning. Remind yourself that you can do it. When you are overwhelmed by negative thoughts, focus on good things. Do not allow yourself to be controlled by your emotions. Words are powerful. How you speak to yourself affects your day. Instead of saying how sad and incapable you are, speak strength. Your mind will start to change and conform to your attitude.

- **Do new things**- doing things that you are used to all the time is not fun. Moreover, they do not challenge your mind to think of new things. If the only activities you engage in are cycling, playing football and reading, switch things up. Start writing, dancing, or hanging out with friends and loved ones. Your mind will grow, and your mental endurance will improve.

- **Be in control**- act as if you are in total control even when things seem hard. Some people believe that you need luck to succeed in life. If your business flourishes, they believe that you were lucky. If you fail, there was nothing you could do. However, do not limit yourself to luck. Resigning your fate to luck is counterintuitive. Not only does it make you lazy but also unreasonable. You have control over your life. Shrewd people behave like success, and failure is in their control. Rather than waiting for luck to determine their lives, they do something about it. They know that they are responsible for their success or failure. Act as though you have total control over situations and improve your mental endurance. You become stronger, knowing that you are responsible for how things turn out. People who resign their fate to luck are lazy people. They do not want to put in the work needed to succeed. Moreover, they do not believe that people can achieve the impossible. Going the extra mile to achieve the impossible builds your endurance.

- **Let go of things you cannot control**- there is no point in worrying about things you cannot control. There are people who dwell on things that happened decades ago. They cannot let go of their failures and mistakes. Obsessing over things that you cannot control is bad for your mental and physical strength. It denies you the chance to become a better person. Do what you can and let go. You may think that you will not get another chance, but that is not true. Better things will come if you let go. Use previous challenges and setbacks stepping stones to brand new opportunities. Learn from your mistakes. There is nothing wrong with revisiting the past. However, do not do it to torture yourself. If you have not moved on, avoid revisiting past mistakes. Forgive yourself and work on your weaknesses. People who have mental endurance have one thing common- they let go. For example, athletes are always optimistic about better performance than previous seasons. They know the importance of letting go of past failures. Furthermore, they train regularly to increase the chances of success. Someone who wants to develop mental endurance should emulate athletes.

- **Celebrate others**- many people think that when other people succeed, it lowers their value. They frown when others receive attention and do not celebrate with them. This is a negative attitude that anyone who wants to succeed should avoid. Other people's shine does not diminish your light. On the contrary, celebrating others improves your mind and brain. Hatred sucks up your mental energy and prevents you from thinking properly. When your friend succeeds, that does not prevent you from succeeding. As a matter of fact, it increases your odds of success because birds of the same feathers flock together. Do not hate other people's success, but celebrate it.

- **Stop complaining all the time... in fact, stop complaining altogether**- some people do nothing but complain all the time. If they are not complaining about their bosses, they complain about the weather, their salaries and the foods they eat. Such people are exhausting to be around. The worst part is they do not like correction. When you spend time with someone who complains, it is only a matter of time before you start complaining. Instead of complaining, put that energy to make things better. Do not complain about things that you can change. It consumes your mental energy. Positivity builds mental endurance because you have the power to make a difference.

- **Learn new stuff** – By now, you probably appreciate that learning is part and parcel of any entrepreneur thirsting for the success of their business. And the best way to improve your mental endurance is to learn new things. It improves concentration, focus, and mind. Your mind grows when you learn new things. You can start a new hobby or learn a new language. You are the one to decide the kind of activities to learn. Learning new things opens up your mind to new possibilities. Moreover, it makes you resilient, consistent. Some people do not want to learn new things because they are afraid it takes a lot of time. The truth is you do not have to use a lot of time and energy to learn new things. You can spend an hour per day on a new concept.

- **Be ready for change**- It is only people who are ready for a change that can build mental endurance. You must be flexible and adaptable. Similar to how athletes adapt to different weather conditions when they compete, you also need to follow suit. Be flexible if you want to improve your endurance. They say that change is the only constant thing in life. If you are rigid, it will be difficult for you to adjust to changes in your life or at work. Moreover, your mind will not grow.

- **Emotional stability**- mental endurance requires emotional stability. There is no way you are going to improve your mental stamina if you cannot keep your emotions in check. Everyone goes through rough moments in life. However, you must be careful not to wallow in your sorrows for too long. It is okay to grief and lament over your loss. Once you are out of this phase, focus on important things. As a leader, you must remain objective and deliver, regardless of what you are going through. Being emotionally stable makes you a good leader and builds mental endurance. It teaches your brain that it can withstand anything. Moreover, it makes you stronger and dependable. When similar challenges occur, you are strong enough to handle them. Emotional stability is essential in improving your mental endurance.

- **Detachment-** you must know how to yourself from your emotions and setbacks.

You can achieve a lot if you know that it is not always about you. There are some people who struggle with letting go. They obsess over their successes or failures, which prevents them from focusing on the present moment. Detach from the past to create room for growth. It also clears your mind to focus on new things. Instead of worrying about your previous performance, think of ways to do better.

- **Be content**- nothing is more pleasant than a content person. This person never complains because he/she has a lot to be grateful for. Instead of being envious about another person's success, a content person focuses on him/herself. He knows that it is not about what the other person has achieved, but what he can do to become a better person. Rather than envying others, focus on what you have achieved. Doing this will change your mind and make you a better person.

- **Standards**- have standards and stick to them. Some people have the reputation of lowering the bar when things get difficult. They accept anyone and anything that comes their way. They do not know their worth and are misused by others. Do not be like these people. Do not lower your standards because things are tough, or you have no way out. Improve your mental endurance by having uncompromising standards. It may be difficult at the moment, but you will be glad you held on when you succeed. People who lack standards never succeed. Moreover, they lack mental endurance to withstand any challenges in life. Developing mental endurance takes time and practice. You cannot wake up one day and become a mentally strong person. You must endure difficult moments and maintain the right attitude.

Positive Thinking and Mental Endurance for business success

Everyone knows the power of positive thinking. How we think about ourselves determines the kind of people we become. The mind is a powerhouse. We can change our lives through our thoughts. The popular phrase "what you think is what you become" applies here. Positive thinking is built on the premise of avoiding negative words in your mind or speech and embracing positive thoughts or actions. However, we tend to dwell on the negative aspects of the mind than the positive. It is easy to find people with a negative approach in life. Some people have nothing in their mouths apart from negative words. How you speak shows your thought process.

Most people only remember a few bad things that happened during the day compared to hundreds that went well. Positive thinking requires maturity and experience to deal with issues that arise in life. It emanates from the mind and takes time to develop. It is hard to develop positive thinking. It is a process that needs self-discipline and commitment. Positive thinking does not an excuse to ignore unpleasant situations in life. It simply means that you handle unpleasant events in a productive and positive way. Instead of approaching them with a pessimistic attitude, positive thinking gives hope. Apart from building mental endurance, positive thinking has other benefits, such as increasing your life span, reduces stress, and imparts hardship management skills. Moreover, positive thinking has been shown to reduce depression and improve physical and mental health. It remains unclear why individuals who think positive enjoy these benefits.

One argument is that positive thinking gives one a positive outlook in life and enables them to cope better with stress. Stress affects your body, and positive thinking helps you manage it. Positive thinking seems vital on the surface. Everyone wants to be positive. However, positive thinking does not carry weight like persistence or work ethics. This is because not everyone values positive thinking. However, people are starting to change their minds about positive thinking. Studies show that positive thinking entails more than happiness. Positive thinking can create value in one's life. Below are tips to become a positive thinker to improve your mental endurance.

- **Embrace positive self-talk**- self-talk includes the words you say to yourself. If you are used to saying mean and degrading words to yourself, it can be difficult to change. Consider this the inner voice that speaks to you. When that voice is full of negativity, it is difficult to develop mental endurance. However, there is hope. Whenever you start thinking bad things about yourself, pause, and consider. The first way to become a positive thinker is to pay attention to your self-talk. If you can control how you think about yourself, you have already won. If you realize that you only have negative thoughts about yourself, you can reframe your mind. Notice the thoughts that run through your mind and assess them. if they are not pleasant, change them into positive ones. Sometimes other people's opinions can cause you to have negative self-talk. When you are surrounded by people who see you as a failure and incapable of achieving anything, it can be hard to have positive self-talk. Avoid such people completely.

If you cannot avoid them entirely, minimize your interactions with them. Some people who lower our value are family members. They do not listen when you point out their behavior. Some may become violent if you challenge them. The only option you have is to minimize the amount of time you spend with them. Block out their negative ideas about you when they speak. You can do this by focusing on other things while they speak. After the meeting, reassure yourself how amazing and talented you are. Honestly, it is hard dealing with negative people. Seek help if it becomes too much for you to bear. Remember that positive self-talk improves your mental endurance. Instead of saying "I have never done this before," say, "It is a chance to learn something new." Rather than saying, "I cannot do this," say "I can try." Self-talk influence your attitude and outlook of life. If you are used to negative self-talk, do not expect to be positive overnight. The more you practice, the more you become optimistic. You will start to appreciate and love yourself the more you use positive words. You can handle stress in a constructive manner when your mind is optimistic.

- **Humor**- it can be difficult to stay positive in the midst of challenges. It is important to be open to fun and humor when things are hectic. Do not be too hard on yourself when things do not work out. Seek out different sources of humor to take your mind off things. Moreover, humor makes you realize that things are not as bad as they seem. Humans have the tendency to take things out of proportion. A simple issue can be turned into a mountain within minutes. This is why it is important to have humorous friends. Go out with a group of friends to unwind. While there, try to focus on the present. Remind yourself that everything will work out eventually. Everything always works out eventually. The next time you are stressed and do not know what to do, watch a comedy or read jokes.

- **Learn optimism**- cultivating optimism is similar to flexing muscles- the more you practice, the stronger you become. Studies show that how you explain things shows whether you are optimistic or not. Someone who speaks defeat or failure is pessimistic. Cultivate optimism by focusing on positive things in life. Pay attention to things that went well in your life. Remind yourself that you are capable of achieving much more. Instead of blaming yourself for things that are outside your control, let go. You can also learn optimism from friends. When you are surrounded by people who think positive, they transfer that energy to you. Even if your mind was filled with pessimistic thoughts, it starts to change. You start believing that there is hope and things can change.

- **Positive affirmations**- repeat positive affirmations to yourself every day to improve your endurance. These are positive words you speak into your life. For example, you can repeat, "I am capable," "I am strong," I" and "I am loved" every day for ten minutes before you go to work. Positive affirmations can change your mindset and make you successful. Your morning determines how the rest of your day will be. Do you remember the day you woke up grumpy and felt like the entire day was ruined? This was because you started your day with negative emotions and carried them throughout the day. It is difficult to be positive all the time, and that is understandable. What is not okay is letting negative emotions dictate the day. If you are facing issues in life, do not let them ruin your day. Positive affirmations remind you that everything will be okay. They inform you that you are enough. Many people suffer from low self-esteem and need validation from people. Positive affirmations remind you that you can achieve anything you set your mind to. They also help you to get rid of negative thoughts and be happy.

- **Focus on good things**- Do not disregard your achievements, however small. Acknowledge what you have achieved to encourage yourself. Do not expect to have a perfect day because it does not exist. You are bound to encounter challenges along the way. However, do not let challenges ruin your day. Recall the good things you achieved at the end of the day to build your endurance. Even if the only that you achieved arrived at the workplace on time, appreciate it.

- **Exercise regularly**- Exercise has been shown to have several benefits to the mind and brain. Exercise 30 minutes five times a week to reap the benefits. Exercise boosts your mood while lowering your stress levels.

Apart from exercise, adopt a healthy lifestyle to retain benefits obtained from exercise.

- **Watch the company that you keep**- the saying "bad company corrupts good morals" is true. There is no way you will maintain a positive attitude and thoughts if you are surrounded by negative people. Avoid people who complain all the time. These are the kinds of people who never see anything good in others. They whine and put others down. If you are serious about thinking positively to develop mental endurance, then get rid of bad friends. While things cannot be good all the time, have friends who are optimistic when they face challenges. You are affected by the energy people transmit to you. Negative people make you doubt your abilities. You start to question things you believe in when you are surrounded by pessimistic individuals. Moreover, they increase your stress levels because you are constantly worried about whether you are enough. Do yourself a favor by getting rid of negative people.

- **Keep checking on yourself during the day**- take a moment to check on self during the day. Assess your thoughts throughout the day. It is easy to assume our thoughts when we are busy. The perfect time to assess your thoughts is when you take a break from work. If you realize that your thoughts are negative, change them immediately. You may have to change your thoughts many times before positive thoughts sink in.

- **Determine areas that need change**- Our thoughts are affected by our behaviors. If you have been engaging in disruptive behaviors, it is time to change. Your thoughts won't change unless you change your actions. Identify areas that you think negatively about and change them. If there is nothing you can do, accept things as they are. For example, if you are unhappy about your weight, hit the gym. However, you cannot change your height, so you should accept it.

- **Writing**- writing has been shown to have tremendous benefits for the mind. When you write down your thoughts in a journal, it frees your mind. A study was done to examine effects of writing on the brain. The study has two groups of students. One group wrote about positive experiences every day, and the second group was given a topic to focus on. After three months, findings showed that the first group of students had improved mood levels, lower stress, and fewer illnesses. This study shows the incredible impact of writing on your mind. You think clearly when your mind is free. Moreover, it becomes easy to achieve mental endurance when your mind is clear.

How positive thinking works

Someone with positive thinking is generally happy, healthy, and successful. Some people consider positive thinking to be nonsense and a waste of time. They laugh at those who follow it. However, the number of people who believe in positive thinking is rising. To make it work in your life, you need to embrace positive thinking in all areas of your life. Consider this scenario; Timothy applied for a job but did not believe that he could get it. He lacked confidence, and his self-esteem was non-existent. He had negative self-talk and believed that other applicants were better than him. His mind was full of negative thoughts in the week leading up to the interview. He expected failure. On a fateful day, he woke up late and grumpy. To make matters worse, he had not ironed the shirt he wanted to wear. Because it was already late, he wore a wrinkled shirt. He did not take breakfast and went to the interview without adequate preparation. He was tense during the interview, anxious and hungry.

He kept thinking about his wrinkled shirt and did not make eye contact. He was distracted during the interview and left feeling worse about himself. His fears materialized when he did not get the job. Philip also applied for the same job. He had a different mindset. From the beginning he believed that he was capable of getting the job. Before the day of the interview, he visualized himself in the new job. He ironed his shirt the previous day, woke up early, repeated positive affirmations, and ate breakfast. He asked the questions confidently and was sure of getting the job. He made a good impression and got the job. The scenario teaches us that there is power in positive thinking. Timothy's negative thoughts prevented him from getting the job. On the contrary, Philip got the job because he had mental stamina.

How Negativity Ruins Self-Discipline

Life is full of ups and downs, but it is not good to focus on the thorns when you have roses. Optimistic people always see the light in the midst of darkness. On the other hand, pessimists believe that people should prepare themselves for the worst. They only speak about their bad luck and how life is unfair. Spending time with a pessimist is a waste of time and energy. When you point out the good in a bad situation, they quickly dismiss your views with bad ones. They see you as someone who does not want the best for them. They will start saying negative things about you to justify their actions. Negative people are extremely judgmental.

When others succeed, they tarnish their reputations. In their minds, they are the only ones who deserve good things in life. The irony is that they do not believe that they can attain good things in life. Negative thoughts about themselves and others prevent them from going after their dreams. Since they do not believe in themselves, they think that everyone is the same. They are surprised when people defy their expectations. Negative people are detrimental to themselves and others. These are angry people who mess everything they touch. Moreover, pessimists are also cynical about the good things in others. If you share with them your success, they will tell you how they did better. Alternatively, they will tell you how someone else surpassed your performance. The worst part is that they do not acknowledge their mistakes. Dealing with a negative person is cumbersome. You cannot help someone unless they show an interest in change. Below are ways negativity can ruin your self-discipline.

- **It makes you lazy**- negative people are sluggish. They believe that nothing good anyway, so they do not put effort into anything they do. They prefer to sit idle and complain about their situation. The funny bit is that most of the things negative people complain about can be rectified with little adjustment. Negativity sucks the life out of you. When your mind is already made up that you will not succeed, you will not be motivated to spend energy on it. You will lack the motivation to do even the things that you enjoy. Where will you find the motivation to go to the gym when you have made up your mind that you cannot lose weight? The body does whatever the mind tells it. If you say that it is impossible to lose weight, your body will not respond. You will not put in the effort to complete the task.

- **It makes you bitter**- when every word that comes out of your mouth is negative, it is only a matter of time before you become bitter. You start to question people's success and whether they deserve recognition.

You start looking down on others and envy them. You feel bitter all the time when you are a negative person. Most of the time, you do not even know where the bitterness comes from. When you allow negative thoughts to occupy your mind, it becomes a habit. It reaches a point where your mind only knows negative thoughts. If you used to be grateful every morning, you start complaining about why it is sunny outside. Moreover, if you used to hug everyone in the office and compliment them, you start avoiding them. Negative people are bitter because they believe life is unfair to them. They wonder why other people have certain things but not them. The first time you interact with a pessimist, you might think that they are having a bad day, only to realize later that it is who they are. They are bitter with everyone. It is not that others wronged them. They cannot control themselves. They allowed negative thoughts to control their lives. Avoid bitterness by thinking about things that disturb you. Do not allow unsubstantiated thoughts to occupy your mind. It is easy to nub negative thoughts in the beginning. If you do not find reasons for pessimistic thoughts, replace them with good ones.

- **It makes you hopeless**- negative people are disappointed in life. Negative individuals do not lead healthy lifestyles because they have no reason to. After all, they will be wasting their time and energy. It seems reasonable to whine and wish for things to get better. Negative people do not see the importance of exercise; why should they? It is not like it will prevent them from catching a deadly disease. They always have an excuse not to work hard, yet they want the good things in life. Negative people lack the momentum to start a new routine.

- **It makes you paranoid**- negative people are suspicious of everything and everyone. They do not trust anyone but expect to be trusted. They become angry when they do not receive special treatment. Before they get into relationships, they overthink about the person's intentions. A million things run through their minds when they hang out with new people. They do not get attached to people easily. A negative person keeps to himself because he does not trust other people. They think badly about others but call the same people when things get difficult.

- **Blame others**- negative people blame others for everything bad that happens to them. They do not take responsibility for anything that happens to them. if they fail in exams, it is because the teacher did not teach well. If they do not get a new job, the employer is to blame. A negative person will fail to put an effort and blame others for it. Have you ever met some who blames people his family for how he turned out in life? While family has a big influence on the people we become, we can eliminate toxic trains. If you grew up in a household where you were not encouraged to be who you are, you could change once you become an adult. Blaming others for your failures in life only leads to resentment. Moreover, it prevents you from living an authentic life. Instead of improving yourself, you are stuck in the past. It also ruins your relationship with others. Because you blame everyone, it is difficult to have friends.

Negativity people think everyone is wrong apart from them. They are the only ones with logical thoughts. Negativity ruins self-discipline and prevents you from developing mental endurance. We all know that self-discipline plays a key role in improving mental endurance. When owning up your mistakes, you become self-disciplined. You know that you are responsible for yourself and other people are not to blame. You forgive those who hurt you and move on. Negativity prevents you from thinking logically. It is not that such people do not know the harm caused by negative thoughts. Some have even tried to stop to no avail. The reason they do not succeed is that they use the wrong approach. They try once and give up without realizing that having positive thoughts is a process. You have to remind yourself every day to think positively.

- **Push people away**- negative people push people away because they blame them for their failures. When you advise such a person, he/she will push you away. They think that you are too hard on them for no apparent reason. In their defense, they push you away. Reasoning with a negative person is difficult because they have a fixed mind. Negativity prevents you from improving your mental endurance. Your mind cannot grow because you are not flexible. You do not accept contrary opinions and see others as enemies. Therefore, you are stuck in the same place. The only way your mind can grow is if you start accepting contrary opinions. It will be easier if you accept contrary opinions instead of pushing people away. It is difficult at first but gets better with time.

People have tried different things to get rid of negative thoughts, but most of them have not worked. Some have tried distractions, alcohol, and hanging out with different people.

Instead of eliminating negative thoughts, these tactics have only made things worse. Studies show that trying to get rid of negative thoughts only makes things worse. The first thing you need to do is to identify the patterns of negative thoughts and step back from them. Negative thoughts have patterns that they follow. Recognizing these patterns makes it easier to deal with negative thoughts. Moreover, it enables you to get to the root cause of unwanted thoughts. Once you identify the pattern, you can step back. The issue is not having negative thoughts, but whether you believe them. When you are not caught up in negative thoughts, they do not have power over you. For example, assume that it is raining, and when you out the window, a negative thought goes through your mind. You start to think that it is going to be a terrible day. If you disregard the thought, it will not affect your day.

However, if you accept the thought, it will ruin your day. It is completely normal to have negative thoughts. Even those with positive thoughts have negative ones every now and then. What differentiates them from negative people is that they disregard unwanted thoughts. They know that those are just thoughts and they are the ones to decide. Recognizing unwanted thoughts and stepping back from them is freeing. You gain back control over your mind. Being in a position to detect anxious thoughts is also critical. They may seem harmless but can grow into your worst nightmare. Another way to get rid of negative thoughts is to stop self-criticism. Some people are their own worst enemies. In fact, no one treats them worse than they treat themselves. They have negative thoughts about themselves. They believe that they cannot achieve anything good in life. Moreover, they do not accept compliments.

When someone says how beautiful they are, they downplay it. There is no way you can improve your mental endurance if you criticize yourself all the time. If you are constantly trying to whip yourself mentally, it is hard to change. Learn how to love yourself. Some people grew up knowing that they are not good enough.

All they heard was how unworthy they are and it stuck with them. Get rid of negative thoughts instilled by others. Treat yourself with care and go after your dreams. Mental endurance requires people who are emotionally stable. You must have positive thoughts about yourself. You can repeat positive affirmations every morning to boost your self-esteem. It is a journey of ups and downs but worth the effort. Once you start appreciating yourself, it will be easier to develop mental endurance. You will have confidence in whatever you do. You will not seek validation from others to make decisions. Self-criticism is another pattern of negative thoughts. Instead of focusing on your weaknesses, commend yourself for your achievements. If other people make negative remarks about you, stand up for yourself. There are some friends who make insensitive jokes and do not apologize. If you have such a friend, confront them about their behavior. If they do not change, look for other friends. It is difficult to get rid of negative thoughts when you are surrounded by negative people. Negative self-talk yields poor self-image, low self-esteem, and poor decision making for your business. It is possible to get rid of unhelpful thoughts if you put your mind to it. Start today, and appreciate the steps you have made. Gratitude is important when trying to eliminate negative thoughts. Mental endurance is dependent on self-discipline and how you perceive yourself.

Time
to think about
SUCCESS

CHAPTER 4: Forming Good Habits And Breaking Bad Habits

One of the wonders of nature is the capacity of the human brain to modify its responses. The ability to change is the underpinning proponent of culture, change, development, moral codes, and above the success of an individual. This chapter gives an overview of the concept of creating new habits or breaking away from bad habits, a notion that has drawn attention for decades. The idea has led many researchers to bring back the perception that the will of human beings is a powerful tool that can be used to control and instill self-discipline in life. The process of self-control links the human body to the mind. In the process, the behaviors in the present and past are interconnected to exemplify the current state of mind.

What traits do you consider desirable? What would you like to possess to make you stand out from the average human being? And what characteristics are essential in making you lead a successful, happy; life? For many years, experts have always shown that there are two answers to these questions. The first one is human intelligence, and the other one is self-control.

The measure of intelligence, also referred to as IQ, is the most crucial aspect in the life of a human. It dictates the ability to understand different situations and adapt accordingly. The same is vital in acknowledging the essential features that one admires and wants to possess. The first step is the identification and the next levels after that are associated with implementation; how to cultivate the identified traits. Learning forms a more significant part of the implementation process. And the IQ controls the learning process. In other words, intelligence can instill a distinct sense of self-discipline that is vital in the daily life of human beings.

The next essential aspect is self-control, which holds the promise of possessing sound mental health and behaviors that can lead to a successful life. For decades, researchers have tried to link self-control to self-esteem. However, the limitations of self-esteem prove that the two, although closely connected, have no joint impact on the traits of humans. This draws my full attention towards self-control as an asset for change in habits, forming good habits, and breaking bad habits.

Self-control is mainly used to restrain habits and desires. To be more exact, the notion is the ability to supersede a pattern with a desirable one. That means that we have to regulate ourselves to possess the traits that are exceptional and get rid of the bad ones. And to regulate, we have to change. More precisely, change our habits towards a given direction with set standards. All this is done based on some personal rules, virtues, or ideals.

The process of regulating oneself can take four different spheres:

1. Regulation of thought. When we sit down and meditate, in most cases, it is always about the concentration of the mind. The process of tuning the brain to shut negative vibes or assume positivity is based on the ability to regulate thoughts.
2. Regulation of emotions and moods. In life, we reach a point where we are low. The right mindset

is trained to come out of the situations in several ways. All the processes and activities of doing so can be summarized in regulating mood and emotion.

3. Regulation of impulse. Desire can be detrimental, and if we don't check our adrenaline rush, we can end up doing things that are detrimental to ourselves and others. Self-control, in this situation, calls for the need to resist temptations.

4. Regulation of performance. One of my fundamental life concepts is sticking by the saying that *it does not matter how many storms you go through, the question will always be, did the ship dock?* This means that we have to work out ways to produce desirable outcomes despite the challenges in the process of doing so. In summary, we must regulate our performance.

How self-control works

Carver and Scheier pioneered an explanation of the concept of self-control. In their work, they opine that the feedback-loop theory is the general explanation of the idea. The theory posits that people will always compare themselves against the standard metrics. If they do not meet the measures, they will look for ways to change and differentiate themselves again. Once they are satisfied that they exhibit the desired traits according to the standards of the society, they exit the loop.

In contrast, I base this chapter on the concept of change. The conventional idea of the power of will cannot be overlooked either. Forming good habits and breaking bad habits is all encompassed in the inkling of change-self-control being at the core. It is a process that acts like a muscle. As you practice more, you lose some energy, get tired, and sometimes quit. But when done persistently, you build up.

People wake up in the morning fresh and raring to go. But as they practice self-control, they consume their power and wear out. Most researchers have shown that the habit gets broken down in the course of the day, especially on a stressful day. This can be the reason why we witness most relapses in the evening. In most cases, temptations are mostly faced at the end of the day, when the body is worn out. This can be a particular case of the marketplace adaptation to the current demands.

Two implications underpin the concept of self-control. The first one is that the process requires energy. From this perspective, we see that when we restrain ourselves from habits that we deem detrimental, we lose a considerable amount of energy. This means that the next time we are faced with another tempting situation that we need to dodge, we find a bit difficult to do so. Most of the seemingly unrelated habits are interconnected in this regard.

Secondly, the power of our will to enact change is limited. This means that when we form a new habit or shun an old one, it takes time to cultivate the shift into our systems entirely. Therefore, a minor effort to exhibit self-control makes a lot of difference in our lives.

Extending the model of strength

I have alluded to the chapter that self-control works similarly as a muscle. And in this respect, it gets exhausted, losing power after use and at the same time build up with persistent exercise. When people exercise self-control for some time, they show improvements in many aspects of their lives. And as Muraven points out, continuous practice improves results in areas where others sit and wait for the outcome.

How can we measure the willpower that people have? In a broader sense, we may find that we do not have that much willpower. Ego depletion and other effects that drain willpower can be associated with limited willpower. This means that the will is depleted almost immediately after the exertion of self-control. However, this concept can be seen as misleading, which brings back the analogy of the muscle. For instance, when athletes engage their muscles, they gradually get exhausted. After some period, they start to conserve the considerable amount of energy remaining in their bodies. This infers that fatigue can be experienced in the early stages while complete exhaustion of power is not possible

In the same way, even if we are exhausted to learn new habits or from removing old patterns from our systems, we will always do so if there are compelling reasons. The most crucial take here is knowing when to give it your all and when to hold back. You do not have to exhaust all possibilities when expecting more challenges and demands to come your way.

Beyond self-control

The processes by which the human body can use core energy resources to supersede responses and regulate habits are an essential aspect in the general sphere. However, the operations have broader applications than the exertion of self-control alone.

Making decisions and choices come at the expense of another activity or event. Understanding the balance between what needs to be let go and the one to be incorporated is essential to eliminate irrational bias. This means that we sometimes duck decisions if the difference is not clear enough. The implication of this is that at the end of the day, what we exhibit reflects the effort we put in place. And as much as habits are concerned, the more the energy, the positive the result.

Self-discipline calls for self-control as one of the core elements, and the combination of habits prompts the discussion on free will. Thus beyond the mere concept of self-control, other rudiments need consideration.

Getting the most out of life

The most important aspect of this chapter is acknowledging the emerging sense of how successful people manage their habits. The popular showing of self-control will power, and general self-discipline fits in the conventional ways of how these people use their inner strengths to cultivate desirable traits that help them cope with crises and challenges.

Habitual self-control is very useful in evaluating the possibilities of excellent performance in every aspect of life and depends less on the power of will, but mostly on regular work habits. Precisely put, it shows the difference between a person who has the willpower to stay up all night preparing for a board presentation and someone who uses the willpower effectively throughout his or her career and doesn't have to stay up all night in the last minute. The difference is noted in the habits of the two people

What needs to be done?

Habits drive most of the activities we take daily. It is the will to keep doing something in a manner that is used to that gets us going. In most cases, we wake up in the morning to prepare for the day, but the routine we have in place guides how our day unfolds. The schedules and appointments are in place to ensure that whatever we do is in line with our desires and work according to plan. That is the mind of a focused person.

For the same reasons that we let our habits dictate what we do, there is a need to develop the right habits. Such developments help to cultivate the correct quantity of discipline into our lives. The questions that we need to consider are where the habits come from? How are the practices developed? What are the reasons behind the on and off of cultivating new habits? And why is it that every time we try to build our habits by either learning to create new ones or breaking from the old ones, we often give up along the way?

The biggest challenge with breaking from old habits is the fixed mindset that we possess. The human brain is made up of millions of neural networks. The neural networks work in the same way as computer algorithms. What we fix the mind dictates the outcome of our actions. We can look at this as a natural human version of training the neurons, just like the computer algorithms. In this way, the neural paths are linked to the neural network to trigger a performance like writing, walking, or walking in a given manner.

The neural paths systemize our daily actions to avoid a lapse in the brain's processing unit, the conscious unit. The automation allows the brain to focus on other vital functions. The process stems from the early development of man, which forms part of the genetic compositions and allows the mind to be used efficiently on other things rather than the repeated behaviors.

Despite the automation of neural networks driving the mundane tasks, the repeated behaviors work to our detriment by holding back the change of habit. In the end, we tend to possess detrimental habits more than the good practices that can help us move forward. And considering that the neural paths in the human brain are deeply fixed on the ordinary over time, forming good habits or breaking away from the bad habits becomes challenging. Every time we try to develop new habits, the old habits block the way. It is the system controlled process that we need first to manipulate before we etch the neurons to our advantage.

Once you can instill the following habits into your life, self-discipline becomes easier. However, the process is a continuous event that takes time to master. Habits take time to develop or disregard, and learning how to create new ones will not take one night's practice. On the contrary, if you set your mind on training and make the necessary efforts to start small and build day in day out, you will be amazed by how far you can go in disciplining yourself. You will probably exemplify the habits that promote self-discipline into your life.

Some of the habits that have implications on the success of human endeavors are highlighted below. Additionally, I have made an effort not only to describe but also give guidelines on how to cultivate them into your being.

Gratitude

One characteristic of human wants is that it is unlimited. We will always want more, regardless of what we have. Gratitude is vital in acknowledging the things that we already have, rather than continually admiring and wanting what is beyond our reach. When we practice gratitude, we notice some remarkable shifts in our activities and lives.

There are vast implications of gratitude. From a personal level, the habit can improve mental health, ensure stable emotions, and uplift spiritual well-being. From a business perspective, gratitude can avoid unnecessary or unlawful competition. The most notable effect is that when show gratitude and are contented with what we have, we gradually move away from the state of lacking something to the state of abundance.

When the mind is focused on what we lack, self-discipline is damaged, and we lose concentration on our objectives. So much of the mental capacity is spent on what we require. This can breed fear. Once we become afraid of the things we want, we focus on negative energy towards them. It is no secret that some individuals or firms engage in black market activities to obtain what they want. Too much focus on the things we don't have can negatively affect even the ones that we already have.

Apart from starting your day with affirmations, it is crucial to spend at least 10 minutes every day jotting down all the things that you are grateful for. Once you note the items in your life, you will gradually feel the need to be thankful.

Forgiveness

Vengeance breeds more problems. And as they say, if you seek revenge, remember to dig two graves. Revenge will cultivate anger, regret, and guilt. On the other hand, forgiveness lets go of many things, freeing the soul in the process.

Without forgiveness, we cannot achieve the intended goals in life; neither can we be self-disciplined. All our focus will be put on the wrong done to us and ways of admitting payback. By forgiving, we let go of the negative energy. This way, self-discipline is natural to achieve.

Forgives possesses clear and positive impacts on the well-being of the self. It is one of the vital traits of maintaining social order, nurturing, and promoting social relationships and physical well-being. Most importantly, forgives is liberating for the human spirit.

Meditation

Meditation is the use of mindful techniques and concentration on a particular sense to train focus and awareness of the situation. The practice is mostly aimed at achieving mental and emotional clarity and calm.

Mediation can be aimed at reducing stress, enhancing personal well-being, realizing peace, and promoting perception. The essentials of this process are limitless.

Mindfulness has a lot of benefits to the person. Apart from improving the ability to be self-disciplined, it also clears the mind, setting the right tone for the day. Additionally, the state of peace exhumed from the habit of meditation is essential in achieving personal goals.

The process of mediating does not have to take long. You can achieve the right state in just 15 minutes. Empty your thoughts and keep the mind still. Close your eyes, and try to avoid any distraction that can make your mind wander. Systematic breathing is essential and feels the air move in and out of your lungs.

Meditation is all about aligning the physical body to the soul. When the right balance is achieved, we can then focus on essential things and relieve ourselves of worries and the things that weigh us down most of the time.

Setting realistic targets

There are two ways of setting targets for yourself. We can set goals actively or passively. Passive goal setting is setting your objectives in mind. They lack a concrete plan and are not adequately defined. On the other hand, an active setting of targets is detailing them down, identifying the strategy of implementation, and forecasting other related aspects. Additionally, an aggressive goal setting is elaborate, definitive, and measurable. When long-term goals are set actively, and we also do the same daily, we make it easier to achieve them.

This method of setting targets gives direction to follow, thus instilling discipline. The benefit of having an elaborate and detailed plan is that it avoids distractions along the way as you have all the processes and steps laid down. When we lack active goals, we become like a ship without a captain to steer the course.

The process of setting active targets means that you must have a long-term goal that you intend to achieve. This way, you can break down the long-term objective into monthly, weekly, and daily goals. The hack is tracking the progress of the long-term goal regularly.

The tracking and assessment are meant to evaluate the progress, how far you have covered, and what is left to be done.

Maintaining a healthy diet

The human body spends about 10% to 25% of energy in processing and digesting food. When the food we eat is so rich in carbohydrates and fats, the body spends a considerable amount of energy processing and digesting it, even when it is not useful to the body. The amount of energy we have in the body is essential in influencing our performance. The power available in the body also enhances focus and concentration.

When we are most focused, we can approach our daily tasks with urgency and discipline. On the contrary, when we are comatose by the food we eat, we cannot achieve essential goals in life. The processes of digestion and food utilization can slow us down if we don't check the type of food we eat. Additionally, we need to understand that certain types of food have detrimental effects on our health. As they say, let us learn to eat our food like medicine to avoid eating medicine like food in the future.

To keep a proper diet, it essential that you come up with a realistic meal plan...and stick to it. The plan should reflect a balanced diet. By all means, avoid unhealthy eating habits, as well as unhealthy foods. Most important, avoid alcohol.

Sleep therapy

The ability to discipline ourselves is affected to some extent to how well we sleep. Every living being requires rest through sleep. Good sleep is an essential part of human living and is an indispensable ploy in a healthy life. Sleep is more vital than you may have thought. We can all recall that time when we couldn't get enough sleep. The dizzy, awful feeling the following day is evidence that good sleep is vital in getting us at our best level of concentration and general performance of tasks.

Additionally, peaceful sleep can help in managing stress, anxiety, and hyperactivity, among other disturbing traits. It is thus essential to learn the best ways of inducing peaceful slumber in our lives to reap the benefits that come along with it.

Exercise

Exercise is an essential habit that promotes growth and well-being. It can make the difference between good and positive traits and the bad ones. If you want to discipline yourself honestly, you will have to make exercise one of your daily routines.

Many people try so hard to get the thing done the right way. However, they fail to understand that staying fit is key to unlocking high potentials. A good exercise does not just keep the physical body fit but also refreshes the mind. By making routine exercise parts of your life, you improve your performance and in the process, build self-discipline.

A good exercise can be beneficial in reducing stress and pain. This is done by the release of endorphins and neurotransmitters, which calms and relaxes the body after an exhaustive training. Another benefit associated with workout is the oxygenation of the blood cells. The process, coupled with improved flow of blood, boosts immunity, thus helpful in fighting disease-causing pathogens in the body. And lastly, exercise helps in sharpening focus and concentration.

Working out doesn't have to be in the gym. You can start by jogging in the morning or cycling to your workplace instead of using a car. Whatever you do, there is always an element of exercise in it. Be it lifting boxes, cleaning the room, serving customers in a restaurant, or any other task. When your job becomes more physical that you get exhausted in the process, take time to cool down. You can consider yoga. This way, this essential habit will become part of your life.

Organization

Being organized is a susceptible aspect, not just in professional life but also in personal life. It is a habit that should be incorporated in everything we do as it gives a direction towards achieving goals. An organized person finds it more comfortable to schedule his or her activities well. Imagine an office where you cannot locate where particular documents are. It does not waste time alone, but also other resources could have been directed elsewhere.

The organization does not end in the right arrangement of items in the office or home. You need to be organized in mind also. You can start small by labeling things in the house and office and arranging them in alphabetical order. This way, you can retrieve easily when the need arises. Doing something little every day is what it takes to organize yourself completely.

Once you have learned to be more organized in life, you will find self-discipline flowing naturally. This can be noted when you start putting things into their own space. The result is the creation of free space that is always relaxing and important for other purposes.

Better time management

When we are engaged in more than one activity, which is always the case in our daily lives, time management becomes an essential tool in determining the success of the tasks. You need to allocate time for virtually everything to get them done effectively. Allocation alone is not enough. Keeping track of the events requires you to be prompt.

The moment we find ourselves managing time effectively, we create more room for other activities that bear equal importance. For instance, the timely production of goods gives room for marketing and sale promotion. If one of the steps is foregone due to lack of time, the entire process is affected.

Most of the best managers of time around the globe are also the most successful people. The reason behind the success can be traced back to the use of time as an opportunity for growth. An example of this can be seen in the difference between people who spend their free time resting and those who use their free time doing research projects. When the two are evaluated, you will find that the value gained over the same duration is different.

Persistence

The little steps you have identified that are essential for your business and person growth will not add any value if you do not follow them persistently. However, they can work to your benefit if you practice working hard in a disciplined and consistent manner. If possible, sweat yourself out to the extent that you don't think about the processes or the effort and resources you invest to succeed. Make it a habit, be it waking up at 2 am to conduct new product research or driving for hours to meet some clients or a supplier. Think about the target rather than the process of getting there.

JUST
BE

CHAPTER 5: Enhance Your Motivation

Motivation is the driving force in any task undertaken. And it is, without doubt, the driving force for success in any endeavor, including your business. Just as an automobile requires fuel to function, so do you need the motivation to succeed in your industry. We require something to provide us with a sense of purpose, drive, and accomplishment. This, in return, helps us move milestones with a vision of achieving the next pedestal.

Just like fuel, motivation does have a price. It is called discipline and dedication. We have to work a way around maintaining it and not running out because we might stall down and halt at the roadside. This detracts the joy of productivity and fluency in our entrepreneurial journey. However, there is a pervasive tenet that problems and misfortunes are the key motivators in one's life.

We are all struggling to stay motivated in one way or another, but this should not be a reason for not achieving our goals. It is mentioned the time and again that whenever you feel like giving up, remember why you started in the first place. It is part of human nature and character to want and find the most natural way out of something. Goal achieving isn't for the faint-hearted. However, there is always beauty and results in the struggles.

The big question is, how do you stay motivated? How do you fuel that result driven guzzler that propels you to your dreams? Just practice. Yes, two words that hold a lot of meaning and sense if upheld with renewed vigor. Motivation is just like your body’s muscles. You require to gradually and regularly putting it to the test to strengthen it and make it more adaptable. Routine practices that keep you motivated have to be carried out and tailored into your work ethical DNA.

If anything, PRACTICE MAKES PERFECT!

Below are some of the ways to set the bar and stay motivated:

1. Have Your Own Set of Rituals or Routines

It is always practical to have something that you do daily and make it a habit. This has to be something that inspires you and uplifts you out of your comfort zone.

You may not understand or know what works best for you, but experimenting is the best option. Some of the key motivators are:

- ***Reading quotes***- Quotes are purely raw facts that tell you the harsh reality of what you're going through, and those have a lasting effect on your mind. They will remind you of your purpose and what happens if you do otherwise. This, in return, keeps you on the edge of your seat and keeps you running whenever you feel like losing mileage.

- ***Support groups***- Sharing helps one build confidence and see possibilities in areas where there seemed to have none. Hearing a similar success story that you could be currently pursuing gives you hope as well as shows nothing but the light at the end of the tunnel.

- ***Listening to inspirational talks.***
- ***Reminding yourself of past victories/successes.***
- ***Reviewing your goals and how much you've achieved so far***.

2. Commit that you are ready to stick with

Being a lone ranger is arguably one of the many ways to lose motivation. We tend easily letting ourselves off the hook in case we face backset or The Great wall of China. Procrastination, in the same way, slithers its way and makes a nest right in the middle of our affairs. Justification and endless excuses for not committing to something follow suit to take center stage.

At this point in your journey, you will need to promulgate and open up to someone. Share your aspirations and targets as well as have someone hold you accountable. Not to mean that you have to report every nitty-gritty to them. However, have a support system that you know will make sure you are moving that extra mile even when the wind blows on your candle.

3. Have a Mantra

Out of your quiver of endless well-polished and earth moving quotes, you can pick out of few characters and develop your mantra. A mantra is simply a statement of principle that you believe in, propels you, or instead defines you. They instigate that positive mindset and passion out of you. Having a report that profoundly resonates with your aura and personality will keep you motivated and hungry to conquer with high spirits and immortality.

Just get a little creative, and you will have yourself a motto in no time. Make it a habit of reading it or going through it whenever you are almost undertaking a task/project or even every morning. This will keep you in check on your purpose and motive concerning your abilities and the constraints surrounding you.

4. Set Gradual But Achievable Goals

Success itself, just like life, is a journey. A journey begins with one step. Let us tone down a little and go back home. Having a small baby develop is one of the greatest joys of a parent. They first have to learn how to walk, then how to talk, and the process goes on. It all does not happen in a single day. The same thing applies to our lives and more so business. We have to start small with achievable and reasonable milestones to mark.

It's all great and acceptable to dream big and even envision bigger but ask yourself, is it reasonable? Small smart goals that are achievable will keep you motivated in the long run and always reignite the sense of purpose. Rome was not built in a day. That is a banal philosophical statement with a clear depiction of our present life. Never bite more than you can chew. You would rather chew more and have a bite of it all. Push that limit every time. Only then will you now that you are progressing. A good example is a weight loss gym workout. Gradual, consistent training gets you to your dream body and not an overnight stay on the treadmill.

5. **Incorporate self-discipline in your day-to-day endeavors**

Let us cut the chase here. At this point in our lives, we are familiar with self-discipline. Self-discipline illustrated is one's ability to tether themselves around specific principalities or moral upholding without supervision or the third eye in the place. Your ability to oscillate around your principles is considered as one of the extensive panoplies of attributes for unmerited success.

Self-discipline is not an innate characteristic. It is a learned skill that has to be exploited and practiced over time. Overindulgence in such makes sure you're stalked on the proper course that spearheads you ahead in the entrepreneurial line of battle. For optimum success, you need willpower and unmatched drive. Self-disciplines will deprive you of your guilty pleasures and time-wasting on inappropriate things.

Its daily application reminds you of responsibilities beyond niceties. Intentional practice is all you need. Present struggles and discomfort though unbearable are impermanent, and at sunset, you'll thank the process. Below are strategies that could catapult you into self-discipline:

Having a Plan

Discipline does not rise altogether with the sun. You require an approach to keep you on course. It could be morning workouts, eating habits elimination of detracting habits you name it. You need active plans that will help you achieve goals and make an impact. An effective strategy is one that will prompt you to saddle up as your life depended on it. So get a plan, you are smart enough!

Control your emotions

Not every day will be rosy with birds chirping outside your window. Avoiding conflict, pain, or discomfort is normal and only sates your present confrontational effects. In the long run, it gets you entangled in a complex web of distress that only weakens your tolerance to calamity. Your soul requires manumission from it if you're tenacious enough to take things a notch higher. So allow boredom, sadness, frustration, and the likes hover over you, and in due course, they'll work in your favor.

Keep your temptations under control

Processing the willpower to shelf your temptations is arguably not an easy catch. Resisting alluring enticements arouses a blood bathed battle between your weaknesses and priorities. A more pivotal approach to it would be distancing yourself. If it is that fries' store at the corner enchanting every taste bud in you, then take the more extended grocery-stocked road home. Seclude yourself from situations that might compromise you as an ossified subject. Starve your weaknesses!

Look At The Bigger Picture

Chances are you have an idea of where you want your business to be in the short term, mid-term, and long term. Orienteering across it is not the most straightforward task, but a blind eye on temporary or immediate gratifications will devoid your future of regrets. Envision yourself having achieved that milestone. Make plans, visit that car yard, enter that real estate dealership firm, and have a smell and feel of success. That will fuel you into making magic happen.

Letting Go of Past Failures

A mistake only means that you never did things right the first time. But it guarantees you of a clear second shot. Errors tend to haunt the living breathe out of you, and will always whisper a defective melody. This attenuates your chances of having a clear goal-oriented focus. Self-destructive activities come in play, but of importance is how you recover from them. Acknowledge a mistake, embrace it, and move on knowing best to do better next time. Forgive yourself.

Have an Effective Back Up Plan

Challenging situations will always arise. How we handle them is what's more important. But what if our first golden arrow fails to hit the target? Do you sob and mummer endless sad orations under your breathe? Before you handle calamities, have a plan that gives you a universal mindset that will prop up your self-control. This enables you to save energy and have a clear mind when making emotional decisions.

Often Indulge in Healthy Meals

A cheat meal is the first thing that would come to mind when you see a diet in talk. Always breaking a rule. That is your self-discipline at stake. Well, you can't function with a hungry stomach. That will often explain that continuous irrigational sensation and grumpiness when things aren't straight. Have you some healthy meals and gas more on healthy snacks. Keep yourself in check for you to run a proper test!

Pat Your Back When Necessary

Rewarding yourself lifts your spirits. It's an esteem and ego booster. With those in check flying high, you're sure of more exceptional performance. Just as you were a small kid, a little reward for making your bed would keep you doing the most on your blankets for that chocolate treat. It gives you a sense of purpose and achievement that hooks you to looking forward to a next win.

Anticipation is more than compelling. The obsession that marinates around it pushes you to stay on the discipline tracks and tweak the odds to your favor. After a giant is slain, look for another bigger one and make sure to reward yourself for your heroism.

Develop New Habits

Old habits, no matter how valid, will, at some point, lose relevance. As daunting as it may seem, instilling new habits could be your one-way ticket to palatial exploits. To make it work, maintain its simplicity. Break it into measurable and doable bits. This will help you mark progress and keep your consistency.

With your goal as the cynosure, make sure they all contribute to your daily development. If it is your sleeping patterns, your waking up routine, always have a head start to keep you on the schedule. A fifteen-minute earlier timeframe on everything will keep you in books. Baby steps are the way to go, and soon it will be encrypted in you. This is something to ruffle up your feathers and get you off your comfort zone. It is in new things that we develop new ideas that help handle the profound challenges that we create as a result of our choices.

Surrounding yourself with the right people

Social Circle

We live in a social world. Biologically we are tailored to depend on one another. From emotional to basic needs. We are operatively after social integration and cohesion. Our surrounding is splayed by different ethical beings and characters that we tap into for growth and progress. The division could be academically, topographical, or even morally. It is a whole spectrum shaded as a cocktail of random societal subjects.

Either way, it boils down individually to your secret society—a specific one that steers your life's decisions and actions. Some are family that you are born into and acquaintances that you acquire. On the other hand —

the potter, guide, and influence on every level possible. Your idea business social circle possesses values and norms that they are principled by. Failure to complying with them subjects you to embarrassment or being ostracized or farther, even failure.

Ensuring you are in a popular clique will enhance your performance and potential in all aspects. Whether you are after career advancements or making friends, you require the knowhow to be palatable. Mastery in making business allies helps you zero in on potential beneficial characters. This keeps you far from spurious beings that might slither deception and failure into your life.

Below are useful tips that will land you the ideal business allies:

Gradually Meet People

Being a social being, get social. Shake new hands, toast to new friends, and mingle extensively. The fact is, not all will fall right in place (or share some ideas and principles), but neither are your current friends guaranteed to stick in forever. Friends are like money. The more you have, the more productive you are. The more value they hold, the wealthier your circle becomes. Cost is the keyword. Instilling value and substance comes from experience and profession. An abundance of it attenuates your chances of failure.

Visit workshops, seminars, talk shows, or even places of interest. Ideally, you will be surrounded by nearly likeminded individuals. Not just in social terms but also philosophically.

Establish on Common Interests

Meeting random people is being sociable. Investing your time in proper sieving will separate the chaff from the good grain. Have a clear picture of the kind of people you want in your sphere. Have qualities, interests, mannerisms, or even traits under scrutiny. Getting like-minded individuals helps you cover more ground as it provides a diversity of ideas and solutions to problems. In a bevy of social beings, be ambitious, and possess an open mind.

Insalubrious characters masquerade. Finding fault in them could be a tedious task. You need to have a keen eye to detail and see beyond the silver lining. As well, relate to what they do. Intertwining with your interests could create high bonds and yet bring value to both parties. Success comes when you all put your minds together. In this, enormous pressure towards goals is achieved since you're all with the same hunger and drive. This leaves no room for laziness because no one wants to be left behind or the weak link.

Reach Out

I mean, do not be clingy. It is often insensitive and uncultured. Yes, be mindful of personal space, but do not drift from your purpose. You won't make a friend and expect them at your beck and call always. Follow up and touch base when necessary. Do not give in to distractions and temporary gratifications. Spryness is what you ought to possess. A business relationship is well nurtured with constant involvement and connection.

Seclude specific days for outings or meetings. Make them feel unique and treasured. Have a clear plan, and if not, at least let your body language makes up for it. Remember, it is not all about you. Remember, it is two-way-traffic. Be present for them and willing to add on to their entrepreneurial cart.

Commitment to Your Community

Cold canvassing could be an arduous task for a reserved individual. Instead, involve yourself in your surroundings. The people around you have witnessed your business growth or failure in one way or another. Engaging with them only increases your chances of a bigger network. Introversion keeps you far from knowing your surrounding's value and how they can contribute to your business. Do not overt hostility.

Offer support and more-so substance. Show your worth in the community. Bring solutions and ideas to a problem or offer a helping hand. Help spruce up the community. Deliver flowers and best wishes to that granny at the house near the big tree. Sponsoring an individual or two and even offering mentorship is highly recommended. Make sure that you have a decisive hand in your surrounding's economy. In this, you will meet everyone. Furthermore, in case of anything unethical, you are sure of people to vouch for you.

Plug into the Connectors

Connectors are simply the decorated entrepreneurs pulling crowds. It could be influencers, brand ambassadors, mentors, name it. An arbiter fits the shoe. Positioning yourself under their brackets assures an audience and potential client base. Remember, you are not making friends for the sake of it. You are building yourself. Adding value as well as learning the ropes. Always ensure to give something back, value. The crowd-pullers are assets you would want in your social circle. Question yourself on which kind of crowds, though.

Canvass a proper strategy that will first get you to your main subject. Connectors will not always make the deepest of friendships, but what they offer is worth the hustle. Ride the wave. Get more contacts and avail yourself more!

Ooze Value

Harking to previous points, this is concurrently present. You should possess a supple personality and an open mind. Acquire a lexicon of principles coupled with proper intellect on essential business principles. Always make sure that the time spent with you is time well spent. Not to include sophistication or unimaginable competence, but have something worthy to offer.

Time, experience, or profession could be a barrier. You might think your more experienced social circle already knows it all. The beauty of it is, you conversed and learned something new in between. On the other hand, having a mentor will help you. They will help you in talking, propping, and even becoming a valuable person. Share your stories, catch up on the latest current affairs, and also exchange ideas.

The important thing is to know their interests and lines of engagement. It is an unconscious tier determined by psychological principles that judges on personal interests. They may enjoy your company or not. It all depends on an attitude tethered on giving or taking value. If it presents itself that you're only around to receive rather than give, they cut ties.

The giving attitude involves putting yourself in their shoes from all perspectives. Be it imagination, feelings, and opinions. It does not have to be lectured on stock trades or market complexities, just simplicity in genuine opinions and judgment.

Benefits of a Social Circle

A social circle affects your mannerisms. The people you hung around with influence you. From your expectations to perspective effects, your surrounding affects how you handle business. A positive surrounding assures of optimism and empowering beliefs. You will view everything as achievable and doable no matter the circumstances.

On the other hand, someone skeptic with a fixed mindset only raises the negative in all situations. A hotshot with a sloppy team of unambitious people means poor results and inconsistency in operations. You will struggle with delayed success and poor performance.

The first step is to identify the weak link in the team and rectify or cut them off. A vulnerable organization is comprised of those with less skill and those not poised for the same vision as you. Spend time with them and understand if you are reading from the same script. If the aftermath feel does not encourage you to take on new milestones and ventures, then move on.

Cutting off professional ties is the hardest thing, but prompt action is required if the value is lacking. Growing together and sharing past exploits and victories could be your salvage point of argument, but your future is more critical than gratification. After pruning, only then will you have unmerited focus and proper sync in your team for a successful business.

Your surrounding reflects on the kind of individual you are. So have a valuable team with moral upholding, a growth mindset, and success-oriented.

Bringing the right people into your cycle

Let's face it: good people are hard to find. After cutting ties, it is best to find suitable replacements that share the same goals as you or of a similar nature. The follows are ways of getting good people:

- **Engage a Business Coach**

A business coach is one with a proper understanding of how specific aspects of the business are undertaken. They are conversant with entrepreneurial principles and will help you overcome backset and limiting beliefs. They will equip you with skills to identify beneficial relationships and those that expose your weakness. A business coach can be a mentor or a member of your team with more experience.

- **Get someone with the Results You Want**

Some people were in your shoes at some point and are currently reaping their harvests. It's normal to want accelerated results, and the only way is to surround yourself with such people. Find individuals that learned the ropes and are willing to help you achieve the desired results. They have a tried and tested formula for success. Spending time with them leads to the skillsets rubbing off on you.

You will be in situations to learn from their conduct and composure how they react to conflict and even forge relationships. Observe them and implement the similarities in your life.

- **Set Your Standards**

We have dreams and ambitions to chase. They all are achieved through sacrifice, hard work, and sheer determination. The question is, what are we doing that detracts or improves the process? What you invest your time in either adds value or devalues you. If you are planning on expanding your business, hang around growth-oriented individuals. They will continuously challenge you to make moves and keep your head in the game.

Your comfort zone could comprise of old habits or friends that pose destruction in your life. The fear of moving on could cripple your ability to focus and make a sound judgment. So prioritize and choose what is best for you and your business. Have people around you that share your goals and ambitions and could go out of their way to see you succeed. That puts your standard on a different pedestal and tests your tolerance levels on various aspects.

- **Attend Development Driven Events**

To get quality people, you need to get them where they lord. Attend corporate workshops and seminars that talk more on business principles. People who know what they won't take a step of learning something new despite its complexity. Expand your mind with knowledgeable material that will expose you to different perspectives and aspects of the business.

Reasons Why You Need More Relationships Than Friends

A friend is someone that you share common interests with and relates to. On the other hand, a relationship is where you are bound by principles and common aspects that benefit both parties. A lone business never thrives, so one needs investors and partners. In private lives, we need friends to maintain a healthy social life. In business, we need relationships in which we will defend and hold each other accountable.

- **There are Never a Lot of Relationships**

The more connections you have, the more credible you are. The more insight you have in the markets, the higher the customer clout. Entrepreneurs admit that relationships are never enough if your goal is to scale up the numbers. Your network determines your net worth. Diversify on your team and cover more entrepreneurial ground in terms of quality.

- **Business Relationships Depend On The Positives**

Exposing your shortcoming may never get you, friends. Instead, it is often used as leverage against you. Keep things professional and only relay what is essential and essential. A business relationship is not one in which you do not splay your vulnerabilities.

- **Virtual Networking Alone Cannot Build a Relationship**

Networking identifies opportunities for growth and legit connections. On the flip side, a real relationship is tethered around personal contact. An online persona can be manipulated and masqueraded. Therefore face facing connections provide authentic, unscripted experiences.

- **Your business partners do not have to be your friends**

Arguably the best business relationships are forged through friendships. Entrepreneurs need discipline to manage contacts and attachments. Keep things professional because you are dealing with customers, competitors, and partners. Some do not have the interest of being friends, strictly business. Friends are emotionally driven to make decisions. Business people, on the other hand, are after helping their businesses and common financial interests.

KEEP
GOING

CHAPTER 6: Build Routines and Habits for Maximum self-discipline

Self-Discipline Strategies

There are several qualities that can directly contribute to someone's happiness and achievements. However, there is only one that will establish sustainable success in the long run, especially in every aspect of life. That is the basis of self-discipline. You can express this quality in the way you eat, how you carry out your physical fitness, and even in your relationships. More so, even at your workplace, there is a way you can express this trait, which will later lead to success in business. In real life, self-discipline is part and parcel of the process you will use to accomplish your goals. More so, it will also help you in having a healthy lifestyle, and at the same time, lead a happy life.

According to Wilhelm Hoffman, anyone with high self-control is happier as compared to the one without self-discipline. In his study, he discovered that everything here was right since self-disciplined subjects concentrated much on dealing with goal conflicts. Therefore, it is good to note that se lf-discipline is not an inborn trait but a learned behavior. In that, it requires both practice and repetitions in your daily life. Fortunately, all these will lead to improved self-discipline, which comes in handy beneficial factors in your life. That's, you will be able to make healthy and sound decisions and not the ones laced with emotional feelings.

In the line of living, everyone would wish to have self-discipline. However, it is not always an easy trait to acquire since it needs time and practice. Its forms surpass many and instill a challenging feeling among those who are trying to acquire it. In other words, self-discipline will always express itself in various types. It can manifest itself in total perseverance, endurance, restraint, or even having that ability to accomplish your plans and goals. However, this will be regardless of the hardships, inconvenience, or obstacles you might face.

Moreover, self-discipline can also refer to self-control. That's the ability to restrain doing unhealthy things that may lead to negative and emotional consequences. In this scenario, you will be in a position to forego some immediate and instant pleasure and gratification to have more satisfying results shortly. However, in this situation, you will require both effort and time to achieve it. Remember, some people always think that self-discipline can cause resistance and discomfort due. According to them, there is an erroneous notion that self- discipline is something difficult to attain, unpleasant, and which demands a lot of effort and sacrifice.

However, the said beliefs about self-discipline are not realistic. That's, the process of attaining and exercising self-discipline can be enjoyable, does not need strenuous efforts, and always beneficial. More so, it is neither punitive nor restrictive when it comes to lifestyle, as some people usually think. Again, it has nothing to do with either living like a fakir or being a narrow-minded person. Hence, it is an inner feeling that resembles the internal strength and power. Therefore, these are very crucial and vital for the achievement of planned goals. And also, helping to carry on with the daily affairs of life.

All in all, self-discipline is a trait that everyone would wish to have even in excess. That's, whether you will have it and go to the extent of achieving all of your goals or being in a position to restrain from temptation, you will realize that you still don't have enough of it. However, the only way to have almost more of it is to get yourself some techniques that will allow you to improve on your self-discipline. Therefore, it will be more important to establish some methods that will enable you to improve on it. Fortunately, in this chapter, we are going to dwell much on various experiments, techniques, and ways which you can employ to improve on your self-discipline. At the back of your mind, you should know you are doing this for the benefit of realizing a prosperous business sometimes later. Below are some techniques that are eventually proven to be part and parcel of this improvement:

- **You have to reduce the number of distractions when you want to maintain strong self-discipline.**

Self-discipline needs focus. In most cases, it helps us in making conscious decisions while performing some tasks. The achievement of some tasks we are undertaking will entirely depend on our concentrations. However, when our minds are far away and thinking of other unrelated things, we might fail to focus. In this scenario, we are allowing some elements of distractions to creep in and, later on, leach away our self-control. Sadly, all the effort we have been investing in this task, without giving in on several occasions, depletes without noticing.

Distractions are always dangerous and lethal when it comes to changing our concentrations. A good example is when you are in a supermarket. Your main purpose here is to buy bread and milk. Your eyes wander far and beyond, then settled on some delicious sweet stuff like candy, snacks, and even chocolate. Unfortunately, you will be tempted to buy these products. Thus, this might lead to impulse buying, which later creates an inconvenience in your budget. Therefore, distractions have got a negative effect on our focus and concentration. They will always lead us into giving in to various temptations. The only way to achieve and maintain strong self-discipline is to clear everything, including your mind. You can also try as much as possible to remain focus on every task that you are undertaking.

- **Minimize your decision-making process.**

Avoid multitasking. Human multitasking refers to the ability to do more than one activity, or task, at the same time. That's performing two or more tasks simultaneously. A good example is when you are driving and taking phone calls at the same time. In the end, you might end up creating some errors which result due to insufficient focus and attention. Even though some think about it having a positive impact on production, multitasking can, at the same time, lead to a drastic drop in productivity. However, for you to realize any success in business, then multitasking should just be reduced or avoided completely. There are several negative impacts of multitasking, which include lack of focus and concentration, memory impairment, increases your stress levels, and also, it is costly to a business.

Sadly, people who assume that they are pro in multitasking are always the worst when it comes to self-discipline. That is, in multitasking, you will be doing various tasks at a go, and this will affect your concentration and focus. In other words, you are consistently and persistently working in a condition embraced by constant distraction. In this case, you will get yourself switching, shifting from one task to another at the same time. Hence, you think that you might kill two birds with one stone at the same time. In the end, your level of self-discipline reduces due to constant distraction. However, the only way to eliminate this is to concentrate or focus on one task at a time. That's, think at a time, then go ahead by doing it. Fortunately, you will not only accomplish more tasks but also you won't be swayed by other bad things.

- **Always make sure you are training the self-discipline muscle**

Most people think that there is no muscle dealing with self-discipline within the brain. However, most studies and findings are showing physical changes within the parts of the brain, especially when these parts do a lot of tasks as compared to the others. Fortunately, it implies that the component of the brain dealing with self-discipline resides within the prefrontal cortex that is located behind the forehead. And in a situation where you are trying to challenge yourself with more tests, you will realize that your self-discipline will be strong. That's, you will be able to overcome various challenges that require self-discipline. However, to make the best here, then there is the need for training brain muscle that's dealing with self-discipline.

You can start by setting up some tests which will put your self-discipline at work. During this time, make sure you are not having your favorite video games or even your electronics, such as phones. You can also put away anything that might lead to distractions as you begin your self-discipline muscle training. Even if you have any form of temptation, try as much as possible to avoid it. Tell yourself you won't give in to anything that will distract you. There are several tests that you can eventually use to train your self-discipline, such as applying the Five-Second Rule and even start small. More so, you can also use delayed gratification. You can also implement the to-do list with three things you would wish to accomplish within that day. However, in this test, you should focus on only one task. Finish them one by one until the three tasks are no more. In this case, you will realize that when you are not being distracted and concentrating on one task at a time, your self-discipline increases.

- **Meditation**

Meditation is a relaxing practice that involves various techniques such as mindfulness and an object focus. That's, this practice instills in you self-awareness and makes you very much attentive in life. More so, it leads to emotional calmness and a stable state of mind. Therefore, in improving your self-discipline, meditation will help you to feel that power of control. In other words, this practice involves sitting and resting instead of having many thoughts lingering in your mind, which might even create stress and other negative emotions. In the end, you will be more equipped to handle the tasks at hand one after another without being distracted.

More so, several studies conducted some years back show that just three hours of this practice leads to stronger self-control and a more exceptional ability to focus. Also, some studies are showing another impressive effect of meditation when it comes to the creation of self-awareness. That's, according to the study, only eight weeks of meditation is enough to establish a greater self-awareness. Thus, leading to better self-discipline.

- **Concentrate on the heart rate variability**

Heart rate variability refers to the rate at which your heart changes when you subject it to various conditions or activities. In addition to physical exercise, your heart rate will still vary during general activities. That's, when you are breathing in, the heart rate will rise slightly and drops a little bit as you breathe out. Heart rate also increases during challenging situations.

A good example is when you are in a situation where the flight hormone has to react. A condition like this will make you flee or battle it out, and your heart rate will rise. However, during this situation, your heart variability will stop. In most cases, this will sabotage your self-discipline, and you will end up doing stupid things that you might later regret.

- **Pause and Plan**

Pause and plan refer to a situation where you have to plan for everything and look for a formidable solution before actions. It is the opposite of the above. In this situation, your heart rate will always drop with the rise in the variability rate. In other words, your heart usually behaves when you are breathing. That's, when you are breathing in, the heart rate will rise and drops when you start breathing out. However, this happens only when there is much calmness assessment during that situation. Try as much as possible to assess your dangerous situation before making a step. Another aspect of this is variability, which can help us measure our self-discipline. You need to note that variability is a physiological technique that you can use to measure your self-discipline. By measuring, I mean, being able to identify those who will give in to temptation and those who might reject any attempt of temptations.

According to various studies, many alcoholics with a high rate of variability were found to stay sober while other groups had a relapsing situation. That's, those whose heart rate could pick up and stay like that after setting their eyes on their favorite beverages. Therefore, in any given situation, whether stressful or not, don't just react. You need to stop and think even if it takes you a few extra seconds of your time. This will help you manage some situations and prevent you from doing something that you might later regret.

- **Check on your diet and the air you breathe**

A proper diet and fresh air will always improve your heart rate variability. In the end, this will also determine the amount of willpower your body can store. Eating cleaner food and having fresh air to breathe in will delete stress on your body. A free-body without elements of depression, anxiety, and even frustrations will have high self-discipline as compared to the one with a lot of stress.

- **Consciously breathing at a slower rate**

There are several benefits of slowing down your breathing. In that, you are subjecting your heart in a condition where you are breathing 4-6 breaths per second. When this happens, your heart rate variability improves. Therefore, an improved variability will activate the prefrontal cortex, which is the part of the brain dealing with self-regulation. In the end, it will create a simple shift of the brain from stress mode to situations of self-control mode. According to various studies, slower breathing for some few minutes can boost your willpower. Thus making you feel calm, being in control, and also, you will be in a position to handle any form of challenges or cravings.

In another study involving drug addicts, a slowed breathing rate led to increased variability. Thus helping in the reduction of the cravings, and even cases of depression will be no more.

- **Exercise**

Exercise is the epitome of good health, and in most cases, many doctors do recommend it to anyone who would wish to live a good life. In a study carried out using students from Macquarie University in Australia, they were subjected to training and doing other physical activities. They trained once for their first week in that month and thrice per week in the next months. However, the results were eventually astounding. In that activity, they were able to note the following:

1. They were not wasting more time and became even more productive
2. Eating junk food reduced
3. There was a decrease in cravings for cigarettes
4. There was a drop in caffeine intake.

Therefore, the above results give us a clear picture of increased self-discipline among the students under the study. Several studies also show that being on a treadmill for about 15 minutes will eventually reduce issues like cravings. This will lead to improved self-discipline.

- **Reduce your time on the news**

No news is good news. And if it is good news, then no one would ever watch it. Media houses are fond of creating only the negative side of their coverage. Anything bleeding will always create a trending situation. In other words, media houses will try as much as possible to feed you much gloom and doom pieces of news, which will glue you to watching. However, to them, they intend to inform you without realizing the negative impact this might create on you. A lot of editions on these 'bad' news make it so stressing up that you will end up with lots of anxiety and depression. According to various studies, stress can initiate the flight and fight response.

In some cases, you can either flee to safer sides where you might think your security is guaranteed. In other words, this might be a portion of comfort food or anything else which might be very bad for you. Therefore, to avoid all these, try as much as possible to watch less news and concentrate on good things which will make your life to blossom once more. By doing this, your self-discipline will skyrocket and improve tremendously.

- **Concentrate on your daily morning habits**

In the morning, your brain is still fresh and not exhausted. Your normal routine of things you need to achieve should start in the morning when your mind is not overcrowded. Self-discipline is high in the morning and steadily reduces over the day. More so, this explains why you are completely exhausted when you are clocking off at the end of your day. That's, you will feel dead and tired on your feet. Therefore, if you would want to increase your self-discipline, then try as much as possible to undertake all your daily activities in the morning.

- **Focus on the reduction of your self-discipline gauge**

In life, when you have high self-discipline, you will always be in a position to reduce your self-discipline gauge. Many psychologists have been testing on the willpower of people. A good example is Roy Baumeister, who works at Florida State University. According to him, the limits of willpower in people can be tested using the following techniques:

1. Shunning junk food
2. Avoid exploding in anger or any kind of stress situation
3. Keeping and submerging your arms in water containing ice

In all these scenarios, students had to stay disciplined and exercise their willpower. However, before this exercise, the same people were involved in impulse purchases; they would also get into procrastination more and even fail to have enough self-control.

- **Concentrate on your sugar level**

In most cases, the part of the brain dealing with self-control, which later on leads to self-discipline, is the prefrontal cortex. This part of the brain always requires excess glucose to function, which it derives from the blood. In other words, glucose powers up the brain, and the moment we use it, our brain works much better. Therefore, this implies that sugar always refuels our discipline gauge. It is now your turn to focus on your blood sugar level and keep it moderately to allow the functioning of the parts of the brain. This will always lead to the activation of the self-control section. Hence, this will lead to both stronger and robust self-discipline.

- **Avoid taking much of diet soda**

Soda diet creates a lot of imbalances in our body system. One of them is an issue relating to body weight. That's, taking a soda diet will lead to obesity. Another problem associated with this diet is the ability to withdraw sugar from the blood for the preparedness for the sugar intake. In the end, the body will have two forms of sugar. In other words, the body has the stored sugar plus the one it absorbs from the blood. More so, when you take diet soda, your body will react by taking more sugar from the blood. This is because your body is getting prepared to assimilate sugar from your blood. In this situation, the body gets tricked by a sweet and delicious taste from the sugar, even though there are no calories. Therefore, this leads to a very low blood sugar level, which is even lower than the usual level. In the end, it creates a negative impact on your self-discipline trait, causing it to be in jeopardy. Also, you will become vulnerable to self-discipline challenges.

- **Only make important decisions when not hungry**

When you are hungry, the chances of having enough energy are low. More so, your blood sugar level becomes very low. Meaning, you will be in a state of weakness. During this moment, your brain will only focus on one thing; that's, your survival. Survival has to be arrived by all means, and this might make your mind settle on some instant gratification mode. In the end, you become vulnerable, and your self-discipline weakens since you will get yourself binging on bad food. Again, you might end up doing things that reflect some elements of low self-discipline. Low self-discipline might lead you to make some decisions in life.

A good example is when you get yourself having financial implications in a casino game or even misbehaving towards your best friend's partner. Unfortunately, this might lead you into great trouble. And because of this, your brain will try as much as possible to save you from this situation. The best thing to do here is to be in a condition where your self-discipline is not in jeopardy.

- **Avoid using "yeah" and begin saying "yes."**

We all know that self-discipline is a trait that you can only acquire through training. More so, training to acquire self-discipline is not hard. You only need to concentrate on a few things that will lead to improved self-control. Simple training calls for quick actions, which lead to immediate results. There are things in life that we always get ourselves overusing. They can be words, phrases, food, or even some malicious habits that we might be unaware of that they are lowering our self-discipline. On most occasions, many people, not only the young but also the older people, have found themselves in using the words "yeah" instead of the word "yes." This has become habitual behavior which always lowers the self-discipline among people.

Fortunately, according to various studies carried out at Northwestern University, the result of self-control was highly fascinating. The study brought about 40 adults who were embraced in romantic relationships. They were later divided into three groups and given different roles. One group was to brush their teeth using a non-dominant hand, and the other one was tasked not to use "yeah" but instead use "yes." On the other hand, the third group was to act as a control group. All this training took two weeks. After this period, the first two groups had a lower tendency, especially when it comes to negative emotions. That's, cases of violence or angriness towards their partners diminished. However, the third group never changed.

In summary, you will realize that the moment you start being more conscious of what you are doing, you will be in a position to improve tremendously. The pause and plan technique forces the brain to indulge in doing difficult and harder things in life instead of dwelling on easier ones. The word "yeah" is always more comfortable in the mouth, and that's why many people use it without necessarily knowing its effect. On the other hand, using a non-dominant hand to brush your teeth is always a tricky situation on most occasions. All in all, you can forever change something that leads to an ingrained habit in you. That's, you can always stop shaking your legs or even scratching your head when you are in a difficult situation. Fortunately, all these practices will eventually help you in improving your self-discipline.

- **You need to go extra longer – you are not weak as compared to how you might think you are**

In most cases, our brain plays a significant role in trying as much as possible to look for us. Our brain will always help us to run away from danger by initiating the stimulation of flight and fight hormones. The brain can also detect when we should stop practicing, especially after training for a long time. In this case, whether we are moving at a faster speed in everything that we are doing will be controlled by the brain. In short, the brain will always look for the safety side of our life. Therefore, this is the same effect that self-discipline always creates in us.

In a situation where we are doing some challenging tasks, we might be tempted to give up and stop it forever. We have all felt like this in most cases; however, with self-discipline, quitting is not always an option. That's, in self-discipline, the brain will always try as hard as possible to amplify its limits. Ultimately, we always make some decisions in life, and at the same time, think and feel what we might feel. However, if we will allow ourselves to soldier on amidst difficulties, we shall cruise on the other side without fail.

Therefore, success in any business always requires steadfast techniques which will help us in improving our self-discipline. Improved self-discipline, together with strong willpower, will still create a successful scenario in all kinds of ventures you might be undertaking in your life.

Conclusion

Thank you very much for having read the entire book. It is my greatest hope that the book has been both educative and informative

The business success not only depends on the physical inputs such as capital and others like labor but also unseen virtues such as self-discipline. Understanding the science behind self-discipline is the first step in achieving your success. After all, everyone would wish to start and run a venture which will live forever. No one would want to start and fail along the way when we are much sure of the cost of starting a business.

The book talks about the power of self-discipline and how it can be used to accomplish business tasks. These daily tasks are the main objective of the set goals. Therefore, to understand much about this, make sure you go back once more to those chapters.

Mental endurance is part and parcel of all business people. Your mind gets crisscrossed every time you are in business. The only way to increase the potentiality of your self-discipline is to look for formidable ways to control your mind.

All in all, the book contains much that we cannot elaborate on here. Issues involving meditation, motivation, and even forming good habits for maximum self-discipline are well illustrated within the book. It is now your turn to dwell on those chapters touching on these.

Therefore, hoping beyond doubts that the book has helped you with enough knowledge, I would like you to share this knowledge kindly. You can also make reviews on other relevant sites since information shared saves a life.

I am...
not how I feel
being here now
my heart's desire
not my thoughts and feelings
embodying my true self
connected to all
the courage I seek
the love I seek
not an object
sensing more & thinking less
a unique individual
fully alive
completely enough
connected to all
inherently valuable
safe from harm
the love I seek
my heart's desire
the courage I seek

CPSIA information can be obtained
at www.ICGtesting.com
Printed in the USA
BVHW061552261020
591850BV00012B/1096

9 781801 123600